LET'S DO A POEM!

POETRY ANTHOLOGIES COMPILED
BY NANCY LARRICK,
Published by Delacorte Press

PIPING DOWN THE VALLEYS WILD

THE MERRY-GO-ROUND
  POETRY BOOK

TO THE MOON AND BACK

LET'S

Nancy Larrick

DO A POEM!

Introducing Poetry
to Children Through
Listening, Singing,
Chanting, Impromptu
Choral Reading, Body
Movement, Dance, and
Dramatization

Including 98 Favorite Songs and Poems

DELACORTE PRESS/NEW YORK

Published by
Delacorte Press
Bantam Doubleday Dell Publishing Group, Inc.
666 Fifth Avenue
New York, New York 10103

Design by Lynn Braswell

Library of Congress Cataloging in Publication Data

Larrick, Nancy.
Let's do a poem : introducing poetry to children through listening, singing, chanting, impromptu choral reading, body movement, dance, and dramatization / by Nancy Larrick.
p. cm.
Includes bibliographical references and index.
ISBN 0-385-30292-4
1. Children's poetry—Study and teaching. 2. Oral interpretation of poetry. 3. Movement education. 4. Music and literature.
I. Title.
PN1085.L36 1991
372.64—dc20   90-44876   CIP

Manufactured in the United States of America

May 1991

10 9 8 7 6 5 4 3 2 1
BVG

Acknowledgments

"Juba Dance" (Creole Folk Song): From THE MAGIC OF BLACK POETRY, compiled by Raoul Abdul. Copyright © 1972 by Raoul Abdul. Reprinted by permission of G. P. Putnam's Sons.

"Prayer of the Butterfly," "Prayer of the Ox," from PRAYERS FROM THE ARK by Carmen Bernos de Gasztold, translated by Rumer Godden, Translation copyright © 1962 by Rumer Godden. Original Copyright 1947, © 1955 by Editions du Cloitre. Used by permission of Viking Penguin, a division of Penguin Books USA Inc., and Pan/ Macmillan Children's Books.

"Two Cats" (Danish Nursery Rhyme). Reprinted with permission of Margaret K. McElderry Books, an imprint of Macmillan Publishing Company, from IT'S RAINING SAID JOHN TWAINING, translated and illustrated by N. M. Bodecker. Copyright © 1973 by N. M. Bodecker.

"We Real Cool" by Gwendolyn Brooks: From BLACKS by Gwendolyn Brooks. Copyright © 1987 by Gwendolyn Brooks Blakely. Reprinted by permission of the author.

For parents and teachers
who have been my students
and the hundreds of children
with whom we have enjoyed poetry.

N.L.

Contents

LET'S DO A POEM!

Introduction
"What I Like Is Doing a Poem!"

NEVER BEFORE have we had so many beautiful books of poetry for children. And never before have I seen youngsters of all ages so happily involved in poetry that they are chanting and echoing lines from favorite poems, even dancing and playacting with the poets.

I have become convinced that this sense of participation is what enthralls them. All ages like the physical involvement of moving as the poet directs and creating sound effects the words suggest. They enjoy the emotional involvement of chanting lines or acting out the role of poetic personalities. As one boy put it, "What I like is doing a poem!"

When I visited his class, I understood what he meant. Soon after my arrival, someone said, "Let's do a poem!" In a matter of minutes teacher and children swung into action with obvious pleasure.

As a poem was read aloud, children tapped out the rhythm or created appropriate sound effects. Or they set up an echo-

1

ing chorus of repeated lines. With one poem they hummed a musical background, which they selected after considerable debate. With another they played improvised rhythm instruments. Sometimes a child called out the title of a poem or simply began to chant the opening line, and others chimed in.

The poems came from such diverse sources as Karla Kuskin, Mother Goose, Eve Merriam, David McCord, Clyde Watson, Robert Louis Stevenson, X. J. Kennedy, Langston Hughes, and the Indians of the Southwest. There was singing, impromptu choral reading, body movement, dance, pantomime, and dramatization. There was complete involvement, and everyone was radiant.

What I saw was an extension of the Poetry Workshop I was then directing at Lehigh University, where graduate students —chiefly parents and teachers—were experimenting with appealing ways to bring young people and poetry together. Very early we came to realize that the modern child's love of poetry depends largely upon hearing the poems read aloud and then becoming actively involved in the musical language of the poems.

Reading Poetry Aloud

Like a song, a poem is meant to be heard. Often the appeal of the song depends on the singer. We are captivated when the song flows melodiously, when the words are enunciated clearly, when the timing and tone seem to fit the mood. Once we hear the song from an appealing voice, we want to hear it again, even to try ourselves.

Before reading a poem to one child or to a group, take time to read it aloud without an audience. That will help you to become familiar with the words, the phrasing, the surprises, and the mood suggested by the lines. Better still, tape your

2

reading and then listen. For most of us it is a shock to hear our own voices, so we have to try again.

We must remember that through radio and television we are all used to hearing trained voices that flow along with assurance and variety.

Most of the poems that appeal to children are very simple and very conversational. Young listeners welcome the voice of a lively reader; not fiercely dramatic, but with the ups and downs of real conversation, or the whisper-soft of bedtime, or the slow-and-scary of an approaching boa constrictor perhaps—always with the warmth of the friendly reader.

"How to Eat a Poem"

As we introduced new material in the workshop, we kept before us the admonitions of Eve Merriam in "How to Eat a Poem":

> Don't be polite.
> Bite in.
> Pick it up and eat the juice that may run down
>   your chin.
> It is ready and ripe now whenever you are.
>
> You do not need a knife or fork or spoon
> or plate or napkin or tablecloth
> For there is no core
> or stem
> or rind
> or pit
> or seed
> to throw away.

So with each new work we bit in and soon were eating the juice with delight. We let no verbal preliminaries or motiva-

3

tion become the knives and forks and spoons that might get between us and the poem.

As new poems were introduced in workshop sessions, we tried out various ways to involve listeners. Before the next week's class, these graduate students experimented with their own children at home or with their pupils at school, using the activities that had evolved in our class or adapting them as the spirit—or the group—suggested.

At each University workshop session, students told how their projects turned out. Even the near-failures suggested guidelines for the rest of us. One afternoon we had two tape-recorded reports of fourth graders singing, chanting, dramatizing. Another evening one young teacher gave her report by leading us, as she had led her second graders, into impromptu two-part choral reading of an Eskimo folk poem.

After half a dozen workshop sessions it was clear that all ages were enjoying poetry as they never had before. Those who had kept it at a distance began to think of poetry more warmly, more personally. They began to let themselves go and reveled in the melody and the movement of the lines.

One evening as we were winding up the workshop, a sixth-grade teacher said: "After teaching all day, I come to this class feeling like a dead duck, but the poetry sends me home singing." I think all of us and the children we met felt the same exhilaration.

Through the years the Poetry Workshop grew in scope. New poems were added to our repertoire, and new poets were brought into our circle. When we had a talented guitarist in the group, we discovered more ways to use music with poetry. And the time we had a former Martha Graham student with us, dance took over.

During these shifts in emphasis and ventures into new forms, we became convinced that initially we all find poetry more appealing when we are the "doers."

To bring about this kind of involvement in poetry means first finding and introducing poems that invite participation, and then experimenting with ways of drawing listeners into chanting, singing, and dancing as rhythm and meaning suggest.

To help you do this, *Let's Do a Poem!* is divided into five main sections that focus on

1) the rhythm or music of poetry
2) the language of poetry
3) the movement and dance of poetry
4) the drama of poetry, and
5) bringing it all together.

Each section recounts experiences with particular poems and ways in which youngsters have become involved in them. Ninety-eight complete poems are quoted, sometimes with children's responses and their proposals for participation.

Once you and your children taste the fun of "doing a poem" and experiment with the rhythm and the lines, I think you will be off to a great adventure that will lead to more reading.

When you find a poet who seems to sing directly to your listeners, it will be easy to locate more work by the same author by consulting the Directory of Poets at the back of this book.

The Directory of Anthologies, pages 109 to 111, is an annotated list of books containing the work of many poets. Through these anthologies, your outreach can be extended beyond the work of writers in this handbook.

All will contribute, I hope, to children's growing pleasure in poetry.

1 Music Has Winning Ways

I LIKE TO begin with a song, for music seems to have a magic effect on children. Perhaps this is because they are used to having it all around them, thanks to radio and television. They hear music upstairs and down, in the car, at the beach, in the shopping center, or riding a bike with a Walkman on. It is the means of communication that today's young people know better than any other; music is in their bloodstream.

Even an infant senses the melody of a song and may respond to the rhythm by bouncing on your lap. The rhythm takes over even before the words have meaning for him. For older children and teenagers, the melody creates a mood and may have an emotional impact as well.

Children of all ages who have experienced this through song seem to respond easily to similar elements in a poem. Frequently those who have listened to and then taken part in singing favorite songs respond with greater enthusiasm and deeper pleasure in poetry.

For the Youngest

The lullabies—gentle and soothing—make the ideal place to begin with the infant.

We have wonderful lullabies from every nation and every culture. Because many have been handed down by word of mouth for generations, the words and melody may vary from one printed version to another. In any form, they provide a lovely way to bring music and poetic language to the littlest ones.

Even though you may not know the traditional tunes of the songs given here, you will find it is easy to read the words in a soft, crooning voice that is close to singing. If you wish to follow the melody in print, turn to one or more of the song books for children listed at the end of this chapter, page 26.

One of the best-loved lullabies comes from Germany:

> Sleep, baby, sleep!
> Thy father watches the sheep
> Thy mother is shaking the dreamland tree,
> And down falls a little dream on thee:
> Sleep, baby, sleep!
>
> Sleep, baby, sleep!
> The large stars are the sheep;
> The wee stars are the lambs, I guess,
> The fair moon is the shepherdess:
> Sleep, baby, sleep!

Many Mother Goose books include what may be the best-known lullaby of all:

7

Hush-a-bye, baby, on the tree top,
When the wind blows, the cradle will rock;
When the bough breaks, the cradle will fall,
Down will come baby, cradle, and all.

Both of these old lullabies become more appealing when you include the child's name as you sing or croon. "Sleep, baby, sleep" can easily become "Sleep, Kristi, sleep" or simply "Sleep, darling, sleep."

"Hush-a-bye, baby," often sung "Rock-a-bye, baby," can become "Hush-a-bye, Andy" or "Hush-a-bye, Leslie."

When a child's distress creates a flood of tears, it may help to bring in the Mother Goose song that begins "Oh, dear, what can the matter be?" It can be adapted easily to the emergency before you:

Oh, dear, what can the matter be?
Oh, dear, what can the matter be?
Oh, dear, what can the matter be?
Betsy has scraped her knee.

And then go on to give comfort through song:

There, there, a Band-Aid will fix it.
There, there, a Band-Aid will fix it.
There, there, a Band-Aid will fix it.
A Band-Aid to put on your knee.

I think you will find that tears vanish as words and melody take over and the child listens for his or her name in the song.

Repeated Lines Make Involvement Easy

Young children are great repeaters themselves. Perhaps this explains their delight in nursery rhymes and songs with repetition. With a little encouragement, they are easily drawn into singing the echo lines or chorus of a song.

Mother Goose offers wonderful possibilities for this. Remember "Hickory, dickory, dock":

> Hickory, dickory, dock
> The mouse ran up the clock
> The clock struck one
> The mouse ran down
> Hickory, dickory, dock

Even very young children will pick up the last line as a repeat of the first and join in with delight. To add to the fun, I often suggest an introductory line, "Tick-tock, tick-tock, tick-tock," to be repeated at the end. My neighbor, age twenty-one months, calls every day or two to see "Nancy's clock" and say the "tick-tock" line to start and finish the song. Pretty soon I expect she will be singing "Hickory, dickory, dock" as well.

Many of the Mother Goose songs invite this kind of involvement through repetition and chorus: "Mary had a little lamb," "Three blind mice," "Polly, put the kettle on," and "Here we go round the mulberry bush," to name just a few. Children love them and soon join in as lines are sung.

The same repetition occurs in many folk songs. These inspire all ages to chime in, first on words and phrases, then on whole lines, and finally on complete stanzas. Enthusiasm mounts with participation.

One of the favorites begins:

Oh, have you seen the Muffin Man
  The Muffin Man, the Muffin Man?
Oh, have you seen the Muffin Man,
  Who lives in Drury Lane?

It becomes very special when it includes the child's name:

Oh, have you seen our Jonathan
  Jonathan, Jonathan?
Oh, have you seen our Jonathan
  Who lives on Cecil Street?

For older children, no song is more popular than "Found a Peanut," sung to the tune of "Clementine." It abounds in repetition:

Found a peanut, found a peanut,
Found a peanut just now
Just now I found a peanut
Found a peanut just now.

Cracked it open, cracked it open
Cracked it open just now
Just now I cracked it open
Cracked it open just now.

Listeners who have not heard this song before quickly catch on to the pattern and join in on the next eight stanzas, which begin:

It was rotten . . .
Ate it anyway . . .
Got a stomachache . . .
Called a doctor . . .
Died anyway . . .

Went to heaven . . .
Met St. Peter . . .
Ate a peanut . . .

Soon everyone will be singing, and before long a few may dream up more stanzas for this old-timer.

The Scottish folk song "There Was a Man Lived in the Moon" is a winner with all ages, perhaps because of the swinging chorus and endless repetition. Even those hearing it for the first time can join in quickly and happily. When they can bang on a ladle, as the chorus suggests, their delight increases.

Take a look at the first few stanzas and note the pattern.

1) There was a man lived in the moon
               lived in the moon
               lived in the moon
   There was a man lived in the moon
   And his name was Aiken Drum.

Chorus And he played upon a ladle, a ladle, a
         ladle
         And he played upon a ladle
         And his name was Aiken Drum.

2) Oh, his hat was made of good cream cheese
                of good cream cheese
                of good cream cheese
   Oh, his hat was made of good cream cheese
   And his name was Aiken Drum.

Chorus And he played upon a ladle, a ladle, a
         ladle
         And he played upon a ladle
         And his name was Aiken Drum.

3) And his coat was made of good roast beef
                of good roast beef
                of good roast beef

11

And his coat was made of good roast beef
And his name was Aiken Drum.

Chorus And he played upon a ladle, a ladle, a
          ladle
          And he played upon a ladle
          And his name was Aiken Drum.

The stanzas go on to describe his wardrobe in terms of traditional Scottish foods: buttons made of penny loaves, breeches made of haggis bags, and on and on. American children love to create new stanzas by bringing in their favorite delicacies. Here is a stanza from a fourth-grade group:

His coat was made of pizza pie
                of pizza pie
                of pizza pie
His coat was made of pizza pie
And his name was Aiken Drum.

They went on to sing, "His shirt was made of potato chips" and, best of all: "His buttons were made of bubble gum."

Another favorite song that is easily expanded with the creation of new stanzas is "The Wheels of the Bus Go Round and Round." Fourth graders introduced me to their version, which grew from day to day.

The wheels of the bus go round and round,
Round and round, round and round.
The wheels of the bus go round and round
All through the town.

The windows of the bus go up and down,
Up and down, up and down.
The windows of the bus go up and down
All through the town.

The driver of the bus says, "Step to the rear!"
"Step to the rear! Step to the rear!"
The driver of the bus says, "Step to the rear!"
All through the town.

The kids on the bus go yakkity-yak,
Yakkity-yak, yakkity-yak.
The kids on the bus go yakkity-yak
All through the town.

The driver of the bus says, "Quiet, please!"
"Quiet, please! Quiet, please!"
The driver of the bus says, "Quiet, please!"
All through the town.

This song lends itself beautifully to small-group singing, one group taking care of the echoes, for example, another the repeated fourth line or chorus, with a soloist singing the words of the driver.

Southern folk songs and spirituals offer many examples of this same wonderful repetition and rhythm. One of the simplest is also one of the most profound:

He's got the whole world . . . in His hands
He's got the big round world . . . in His hands
He's got the wide world . . . in His hands
He's got the whole world in His hands.

He's got the wind and the rain . . . in His
   hands
He's got the sun and the moon . . . in His
   hands
He's got the wind and the rain . . . in His
   hands
He's got the whole world in His hands.

He's got you and me, brother . . . in His hands
He's got you and me, sister . . . in His hands

13

He's got everybody . . . in His hands
He's got the whole world in His hands.

What else? Some of the children's suggestions:

The snow and the ice . . .
The rabbits and the squirrels . . .
The rivers and the streams . . .
My mother and the baby . . .
The teacher and the children . . . and on and
on.

And each time singers return to the old stanzas or the newly created ones, they are experiencing rhythmical language of which they are a part.

A bit more complicated, but equally popular, is "One Wide River to Cross," the spiritual about loading animals on Noah's Ark before the flood. It suggests countless variations:

1) Old Noah built himself an Ark
One wide river to cross
He built it out of hickory bark
One wide river to cross.

Chorus One wide river and that wide river
is Jordan
One wide river, just one wide river
to cross.

2) The animals came in one by one
One wide river to cross
And Japheth played his big bass drum
One wide river to cross.

Chorus One wide river and that wide river
is Jordan

One wide river, just one wide river
to cross.

3) The animals came in two by two
One wide river to cross
The alligator and the kangaroo
One wide river to cross.

Chorus One wide river and that wide river
is Jordan
One wide river, just one wide river
to cross.

The stanzas go on and on, changing as the singers determine. Some of the versions I have heard are:

The animals came in three by three
The woolly bear and the honeybee.

Chorus

The animals came in four by four
The billy goats clattered across the floor

Chorus

The animals came in five by five
The elephant muttered, "Sakes alive!"

Chorus

Two ten-year-olds came up with these stanzas:

The animals came in six by six
The big baboon was doing tricks.

Chorus

The animals came in eight by eight
The donkeys came by roller skate.

Chorus

15

And so it goes until Noah packs them all in or inventive singers give up.

I have found that children become engrossed in the rhythm and repetition as well as in the challenge to add more and more stanzas. Play with words and play with rhythm seem to build greater pleasure in the music of language.

Of the spirituals, none is more appealing to middle graders than "Kum ba ya," once they get into the swing of the very simple language. Each stanza introduces just one new word —*crying, singing, praying,* for example—but that word determines the mood and hence the tempo of the whole stanza.

> *Chorus* Kum ba ya, my Lord, Kum ba ya!
> Kum ba ya, my Lord, Kum ba ya!
> Oh, Lord, Kum ba ya!
>
> Someone's crying, Lord, Kum ba ya!
> Someone's crying, Lord, Kum ba ya!
> Someone's crying, Lord, Kum ba ya!
> Oh, Lord, Kum ba ya!
>
> *Chorus*
>
> Someone's singing, Lord, Kum ba ya!
> Someone's singing, Lord, Kum ba ya!
> Someone's singing, Lord, Kum ba ya!
> Oh, Lord, Kum ba ya!
>
> *Chorus*
>
> Someone's praying, Lord, Kum ba ya!
> Someone's praying, Lord, Kum ba ya!
> Someone's praying, Lord, Kum ba ya!
> Oh, Lord, Kum ba ya!

Children who have had experience creating new stanzas for an old song are quick to suggest additional key words:

playing, dancing, weeping, for example, even *giggling.* But the tempo must vary with the word, they find. A quick, joyous rhythm is more appropriate for *dancing* and a slow, plaintive rhythm for *weeping.* So without detailed lessons, youngsters learn that the rhythm of the poem is in harmony with the mood. Together they create an emotional impact on readers and listeners.

I will never forget being in a fifth-grade class where children were spinning out one stanza after another of "Kum ba ya." Without previous assignment, one child would take the solo part and sing out "Someone's happy, Lord" or "Someone's laughing, Lord." Immediately the class would complete the rest of the stanza, changing the tempo to fit the mood.

One day a child sang out: "Someone's lonely, Lord." This was a new concept, but at once the class picked up her suggestion and sang through the stanza in tender tones. Later the teacher told me that this youngster was new in the group and up to this point seemed to keep to herself. Lonely. Of course. Quickly her classmates seemed to get the message from the song. They sensed her need and took her in.

Songs That Call for an Echo

In many of these old songs repeated words or phrases can be treated like an echo or a series of echoes, sung by one or more voices. Remember the chorus of "There Was a Man Lived in the Moon":

> And he played upon a ladle, a ladle, a ladle
> He played upon a ladle
> And his name was Aiken Drum.

One person can sing or chant the first part, "And he played upon a ladle." Another can echo the words "a ladle," and a third can come in with an even softer, more distant echo, with everybody joining in on the next two lines. As more and more children are drawn into the song, it gains interest and drama.

"Miss Mary Mack, Mack, Mack" is another folk song that seems made for echoing whether you sing the old tune or simply chant the words.

Each line follows the pattern of the first:

Miss Mary Mack, Mack, Mack

Parcel out echo privileges to two singers or two small groups and plunge in, with the echoes taking care of the last two words in each line.

Miss Mary Mack, Mack, Mack
All dressed in black, black, black
With silver buttons, buttons, buttons,
All down her back, back, back.

She asked her mother, mother, mother
For fifteen cents, cents, cents,
To see the elephant, elephant, elephant
Jump the fence, fence, fence.

He jumped so high, high, high
That he touched the sky, sky, sky
And never came back, back, back
Till the Fourth of July, July, July.

Frequently singers like to emphasize the beat of the last three words in each line by clapping as they sing.

Another old song, perfect for echoing and improvising, begins, "Oh, you can't get to heaven." The stanzas below have come from a variety of sources. By this time, I am not sure which are the traditional stanzas and which have been created by the kids themselves.

Solo: Oh, you can't get to   *Echo:* You can't get to
    heaven   heaven
    In a rocking chair   In a rocking chair
    'Cause a rocking   a rocking chair
      chair   won't get you there.
    Won't get you there.

Chorus (all together)

    You can't get to heaven in a rocking chair
    'Cause a rocking chair won't get you there
    But I ain't gonna grieve, my Lord, no more
    Ain't gonna grieve, my Lord, no more.

If your echo group is on the alert, there will probably be a call to repeat the fourth line of the chorus as another echo. More fun for all!

Among the stanzas I have heard:

    Oh, you can't get to heaven on roller skates
    'Cause you'll roll right by St. Peter's gates.

    Oh, you can't get to heaven on a rocket ship
    'Cause a rocket ship won't make the trip.

    Oh, you can't get to heaven with Superman
    'Cause our good Lord is a Batman fan.

    Oh, you can't get to heaven in Butch's car
    'Cause his old wreck won't go that far.

Many popular camp songs have this same kind of repetition and chorus, which invite two-group singing. One of the favorites is built on the echo principle, which makes involvement very easy:

NANCY LARRICK

SIPPIN' CIDER THROUGH A STRAW

Group: The cutest boy   *Echo:* the cutest boy
I ever saw   I ever saw
Was sippin' cider   was sippin' cider
Through a straw   through a straw

I walked right in   I walked right in
And sat right down   and sat right down
And got a cider   and got a cider
But not a straw   but not a straw

I inched my way   I inched my way
Across the seat   across the seat
And hoped by   and hoped by
  chance   chance
That we could   that we could
  meet   meet

I smiled at him   I smiled at him
He smiled at me   he smiled at me
We would be   we would be
  friends   friends
'Twas plain to see   'twas plain to see

The cutest boy   the cutest boy
I ever saw   I ever saw
Let me sip cider   let me sip cider
Through his straw   through his straw

First cheek to   first cheek to
  cheek   cheek
Then jaw to jaw   then jaw to jaw
We both sipped   we both sipped
  cider   cider
Through a straw   through a straw

20

And all at once   and all at once
The straw did slip   the straw did slip
Then we sipped   then we sipped
   cider   cider
Lip to lip   lip to lip

Now 16 kids   now 16 kids
All call me "Ma"   all call me "Ma"
From sippin' cider   from sippin' cider
Through a straw   through a straw

And all because   and all because
the cutest boy   the cutest boy
I ever saw   I ever saw
Was sippin' cider   was sippin' cider
Through a straw   through a straw.

"She'll Be Comin' Round the Mountain" seems ready-made for an echo or two as well as a chorus. To add to the fun, singers often create new stanzas to fit the established pattern. Instead of the familiar line "She'll be drivin' six white horses when she comes," they love to sing: "She'll be ridin' a Suzuki when she comes." Then for the finale, like a mournful dirge: "She'll be ridin' in a hearse when she goes."

Songs That Call for Sound Effects

For younger children, in particular, there is great charm in songs that create sound effects or imitate animal voices. "Old McDonald Had a Farm" is typical, with the opportunity to add the voice of the cat, the pig, the cow, the sheep, the dog, or whatever animals the singers choose to add to the assortment. One group of sixth graders varied their list by adding pieces of farm equipment with appropriate whangs and twangs, sputters and rumbles, for a chain saw, a pick-up truck, and a mower.

21

Not quite so well known but offering the same opportunity to create sound effects is "Bought Me a Cat," a folk song that I first heard on an early Pete Seeger recording:

> Bought me a cat, the cat pleased me.
> I fed my cat under yonder tree.
> The cat went fiddle-i-fee, fiddle-i-fee.
>
> I bought me a hen, the hen pleased me.
> I fed my hen under yonder tree.
> The hen went chipsy, chopsy
> The cat went fiddle-i-fee.
>
> I bought me a dog, the dog pleased me.
> I fed my dog under yonder tree.
> The dog went bow-wow
> The hen went chipsy-chopsy
> The cat went fiddle-i-fee.

As the singer buys and then feeds a goose, a duck, a sheep, a cow, a horse, and all the rest, the animal voices increase in number and singers sound like a veritable barnyard chorus, growing more realistic with every round.

The absolute winner—with grown-ups as well as children—is "The Little Bullfrog Song." Whether words are sung or chanted, the throaty "glunks" and "gloops" get everybody into the act. The words—and the tune—are simple enough, but singers can make it sound like an all-frog choral society in top performance.

> *Glunk glunk* went the little bullfrog one day.
> *Glunk glunk* went the little bullfrog.
> *Glunk glunk* went the little bullfrog one day
> And his eyes went *gloop gloop gloop*.

"The Merry-Go-Round Song" suggests very different sound effects for the up-and-down tootle of the old-fashioned carousel, which has delighted youngsters for generations. The words and music are easy to introduce for group singing:

> The more we get together
> Together, together
> The more we get together
> The happier we'll be.
>
> For your friends are my friends
> And my friends are your friends
> The more we get together
> The happier we'll be.

The real fun begins when the sound-effects team imitates the music of the merry-go-round as background for the words sung by the other children.

For this there should be three sound-effects people or three small sound-effects groups.

One will repeat the sounds *OOM-pa-pa, OOM-pa-pa* over and over in a deep bass as the first stanza of the song begins.

The second will come in on the next stanza an octave higher—*OOM-siss-siss, OOM-siss-siss*—while the bass chorus continues.

As the first stanza is repeated, the third group will join in on a high soprano, *OOM-tweedle-dee, OOM-tweedle-dee.* Singers and the three sound-effect groups will all continue through the second stanza.

As stanzas are repeated, one sound-effects group after another drops out: first the bass, then on the next, the middle range. Finally the high *OOM-tweedle-dee* carries on alone. This is a performance everyone wants to repeat again and again.

Songs That Tell a Story

All ages seem to be ready for a story on any occasion. If it is a story in song, so much the better. For the very young, Mother Goose provides simple narratives in song: Jack and Jill, Humpty Dumpty, Little Miss Muffet, Little Bo-peep, and dozens more. I think these are popular because each immediately names the protagonists (Jack and Jill, for example), gives the setting ("went up the hill"), states the purpose ("to fetch a pail of water"), and explains the outcome ("Jack fell down," etc.). In just two four-line stanzas, the tale is told.

Listeners are satisfied and quickly ask for a repeat. The melody is as simple as the words, so it is easy for a young child to chime in after hearing it only a few times. Often it is fun for you and the child to sing alternate lines.

In such a Mother Goose song as "Pussy Cat, Pussy Cat," you may want to make the most of the question-and-answer pattern with you asking the questions and the child replying:

> Pussy cat, pussy cat, where have you been?
> I've been to London to visit the queen.
> Pussy cat, pussy cat, what did you there?
> I frightened a little mouse under her chair.

Middle graders will plunge happily into the questions and answers of the folk song that begins "Where are you going to, my pretty maid?" (also a part of Mother Goose). This is great fun when one singer asks the questions, another gives the answers of the milkmaid (lines two and four), and others in the group sing the repeated words "sir, she said."

> Where are you going to, my pretty maid?
> I'm going a-milking, sir, she said,
> Sir, she said, sir, she said,
> I'm going a-milking, sir, she said.

May I go with you, my pretty maid?
You're kindly welcome, sir, she said,
Sir, she said, sir, she said,
You're kindly welcome, sir, she said.

Say, will you marry me, my pretty maid?
Yes, if you please, kind sir, she said,
Sir, she said, sir, she said,
Yes, if you please, kind sir, she said.

What is your fortune, my pretty maid?
My face is my fortune, sir, she said,
Sir, she said, sir, she said,
My face is my fortune, sir, she said.

Then I can't marry you, my pretty maid.
Nobody asked you, sir, she said,
Sir, she said, sir, she said,
Nobody asked you, sir, she said.

From Songs to Poetry

If we listen to a song again and again and are drawn into
some sort of participation, the music seems to become a part
of us, and the mood of the song takes over.

Softly, tenderly, for the stanza that begins "Someone's crying, Lord" in "Kum ba ya." Glunking and glooping for "The
Little Bullfrog Song." Coy and flirtatious for "Sippin' Cider."
First coquettish and then with a quick snap-off in "Where are
you going to, my pretty maid?"

With this experience, we are better able to lose ourselves in
the mood and the melody of a poem. We become sensitive to
rhythm and begin to feel these differences in poetry more
easily because we have felt them in songs.

Song Books
for Children

(All include words and musical notations.)

Collections of Songs

American Folk Songs for Children, compiled by Ruth Craw-
ford Seeger. A splendid collection by a great teacher of
music. Doubleday, 1948. Paperback.

*Arroz con Leche: Popular Songs and Games from Latin Amer-
ica,* selected and illustrated by Lulu Delacre; English lyrics
by Elena Paz. Lyrics for a dozen songs and folk games from
Puerto Rico, Mexico, and Argentina in both Spanish and
English. Scholastic, 1989.

Every Child's Book of Nursery Songs, selected by Donald
Mitchell. Ninety-one nursery rhymes with simple piano arrangements. Published in Great Britain as *The Faber Book
of Nursery Songs* by Faber & Faber. London, 1958. Published in the U.S. as *Every Child's Book of Nursery Rhymes*
by Crown Publishers. 1985. Paperback.

The Fireside Book of Children's Songs, compiled by Marie

Winn and Allan Miller. More than 100 of the finest and most beautiful. Simon & Schuster, 1966.

The Fireside Book of Fun and Game Songs, compiled by Marie Winn. Simon & Schuster, 1974.

Go in and out the Window: An Illustrated Songbook for Young People. Sixty-one classic childhood songs with illustrations in full color from treasures of the Metropolitan Museum of Art. The Metropolitan Museum of Art and Henry Holt & Co., 1987.

If You're Happy and You Know It: Eighteen Story Songs, set to pictures by Nicki Weiss. Greenwillow, 1987.

Lullabies and Night Songs, edited by William Engvick; music by Alec Wilder; illustrations by Maurice Sendak. Forty-six lullabies and songs with simple melodies and arrangements. Harper & Row, 1965.

The Lullaby Song Book, edited by Jane Yolen; musical arrangements by Adam Stemple. Fifteen cherished lullabies with music and exquisite illustrations. Harcourt Brace Jovanovich, 1986.

Singing Bee! A Collection of Favorite Children's Songs, edited by Jane Hart; illustrated by Anita Lobel. Lothrop, Lee & Shepard, 1982.

Skipping to Babylon: A Collection of Skipping Rhymes, collected and illustrated by Carole Tate. Delightful illustrations for amusing old rhymes. Oxford University Press, 1985.

Songs from Mother Goose. Fifty-six Mother Goose rhymes with simple musical notations for the old melodies. Compiled by Nancy Larrick; illustrated by Robin Spowart. Harper & Row, 1989.

Thirty Old-Time Nursery Songs, arranged by Joseph Moorat and pictured by Paul Woodroffe. First published in England in 1912, this new edition has been produced from the original watercolor illustrations, musical notations, and handwritten text. The Metropolitan Museum of Art and Thames & Hudson, 1980.

Tom Glazer's Treasury of Songs for Children, edited by Tom Glazer. Doubleday, 1988.

Walk Together Children: Black American Spirituals, selected and illustrated by Ashley Bryan. Twenty-four songs with music and stunning woodcuts. Macmillan, 1974.

What a Morning! The Christmas Story in Black Spirituals, compiled by John Langstaff; illustrated by Ashley Bryan. Macmillan, 1987.

Each Book a Single Song

Always Room for One More, edited by Sorche Nic Leodhas; illustrated by Nonny Hogrogian. A single Scottish song with music. Henry Holt, 1965. Paperback.

The Fox Went Out on a Chilly Night. A beloved folk song with music arranged by Burl Ives. Illustrated by Peter Spier. Doubleday, 1961

Frog Went a-Courtin', retold by John Langstaff. A favorite folk song transformed into a picture book with music. Harcourt, Brace & Jovanovitch, 1955.

Once: A Lullaby by bp Nichol; illustrated by Anita Lobel; music by Adam Lobel. Eighteen rhythmical stanzas with delightful repetition and humor. Text copyright 1986 by bp Nichol; illustrations copyright 1986 by Anita Lobel. Greenwillow Books, 1986.

Over in the Meadow, edited by John Langstaff; illustrated by Feodor Rojankowsky. Verses of an old counting song with music. Harcourt Brace Jovanovich, 1967. Paperback.

2 When Two or More Read Aloud

ONE OF THE most effective ways by which a child can become involved in poetry is through reading aloud or chanting with someone else or with a small group. Creating the sounds of poetry seems to have special appeal to kids growing up in our auditory world. Even nonreaders easily pick up repeated words and chime in on cue. All seem to enjoy the sense of participation and are quickly drawn into the rhythm and meaning of the words. It becomes spur-of-the-moment choral reading for immediate pleasure.

This should not be confused with the formal choral reading of bygone years when selected children were rehearsed with the precision of the school glee club. Instead, this is spontaneous, with solo parts taken as the situation suggests. One individual or small group may agree in advance to read or chant the repeated lines or chorus. Another may ask to take over the chorus on the next go-round while the first hums a background melody. Solo voices may chime in spontaneously, as they did with the song "Kum ba ya." In one poem, new lines may be created on the pattern of the old. In another, two voices may read alternate lines or echo repeated words or phrases.

Many of the practices used in group singing are equally effective with group reading.

Poems with a Chorus

Any poem with a chorus invites participation of readers and nonreaders alike. Even the shy ones gain assurance. When the same line is repeated according to a regular pattern, each realizes it is easy to join in and become a part of it all.

As a starter with young children, I often choose one of the poetic chants by Bill Martin Jr. This is one of their favorites.

INDIAN CHANT

(to be read like the beat of a tom-tom)

Beat beat
Beat upon the tom-tom
Beat beat
Beat upon the drum
Beat beat
Beat upon the tom-tom
Beat beat
Beat upon the drum

Shuffle to the left
Shuffle to the left
Shuffle shuffle
Shuffle shuffle
Shuffle to the left

Beat beat
Beat upon the tom-tom

Beat beat
Beat upon the drum.

Children love to get on their feet, chant the "Beat beat" lines, and move to the "Shuffle shuffle" lines. A real drum— or several of them—and a tom-tom or improvised instruments add to the effect.

At Halloween, Bill Martin's "Witches' Chant" is too good to miss.

WITCHES' CHANT

(to be read like the beat of a tom-tom)

One little, two little,
Three little witches,
Flying over haystacks,
Flying over ditches,
Sliding down moonbeams.
Wearing out their britches.
Hi Ho
Halloween's here!

Shuffle to the left,
Shuffle to the left,
Shuffle shuffle
Shuffle shuffle
Shuffle to the left.

One little, two little,
Three little witches,
Hi Ho
Halloween's here!

Read it aloud, and on the next go-round I think you will find your listeners are eager to join you on repeated lines such as

One little, two little,
Three little witches . . .

and later on

Hi Ho
Halloween's here!

If you are reading to several children, you will surely have volunteers to act out the role of the three little witches while others chant the lines to the beat of a tom-tom.

Another favorite is the folk poem about making a Christmas pudding. It has a vigorous chorus in the second line of each couplet. If you take the first line in each stanza, children will enjoy chanting the second, possibly with lively stirring motions as well.

Into the basin put the plums,
Stirabout, stirabout, stirabout!

Next the good white flour comes,
Stirabout, stirabout, stirabout!

Sugar and peel and eggs and spice.
Stirabout, stirabout, stirabout!

Mix them and fix them and cook them twice.
Stirabout, stirabout, stirabout!

Two recent books for younger children provide wonderful opportunities for reading aloud together. Each is a long poem with rhythmical stanzas setting a pattern of repetition that invites a child's involvement. Read a few stanzas aloud, and your listener will soon be chiming in.

One of these picture-book poems is *Once: A Lullaby*, written by bp Nichol and illustrated by Anita Lobel. It begins:

Once I was a little horse,
baby horse, little horse.
Once I was a little horse.
NEIGH, I fell asleep.

Once I was a little cow,
baby cow, little cow.
Once I was a little cow.
MOO, I fell asleep.

Once I was a little goat . . .

And so it goes for eighteen stanzas with sheep, pig, dog, cat, and all the rest falling asleep. Children love it.

The second book, also a one-poem picture-book, is *Tickle-Toe Rhymes* by Joan Knight, illustrated by John Wallner. It might be described as a one-to-five counting book with the ridiculous doings of various animals shown in delightfully detailed pictures. The first three stanzas reveal the pattern followed throughout—easy enough for a very young child to take over as his own.

I find it is a good plan to have children recite the first half of each line:

One little piggie . . .
Two little piggies . . .
Three little piggies . . . and so on.

Then I complete each line by reading the printed script. This kind of partnership becomes a sort of game for all to take part in.

TICKLE-TOE RHYMES

One little piggie wore leggings,
Two little piggies wore wigs,
Three little piggies wore bustles,

Four little piggies did jigs,
Five little piggies wore nothing at all,
And said that the others were prigs.

One little kid took a limo,
Two little kids took a bus,
Three little kids took a buggy,
Four little kids made a fuss,
Five little kids created a stir,
Crying, "Nanny, what about *us*?"

One little bunny grew carrots,
Two little bunnies grew greens,
Three little bunnies grew mushrooms,
Four little bunnies grew beans,
Five little bunnies pickled them all
And served them in cabbage tureens.

In Margaret Wise Brown's poem "Old Snake Has Gone to
Sleep," the chorus is a gentle melody for a quiet scene. Children respond to the mood and like to chant the chorus. By
the end they are almost whispering "Old snake has gone to
sleep."

Sun shining bright on the mountain rock
Old snake has gone to sleep.
Wild flowers blooming round the mountain
    rock
Old snake has gone to sleep.
Bees buzzing near the mountain rock
Old snake has gone to sleep.
Sun shining warm on the mountain rock
Old snake has gone to sleep.

David McCord's "Riddle-Me Rhyme" really has two choruses:

Riddle-me, Riddle-me, Ree, *and*
Riddle-me, Riddle-me, Ro.

First one, and then the other, sings out through the tale of an
owl beset by crows. As you read the story lines, it is fun to
have two children repeat the choruses alternately. Or they
may choose to form a small chorus for each.

RIDDLE - ME RHYME

Riddle-me, Riddle-me, Ree,
An owl is in that tree.
Riddle-me, Riddle-me, Ro,
He's there and he won't go.
Riddle-me, Riddle-me, Ree,
"I'm staying here," says he.
Riddle-me, Riddle-me, Ro,
"Caw-caw," caws the crow.
Riddle-me, Riddle-me, Ree,
An owl by day can't see.
Riddle-me, Riddle-me, Ro,
But he can hear the crow.
Riddle-me, Riddle-me, Ree,
Not *one* crow: now but three.
Riddle-me, Riddle-me, Ro,
Now five or six or so.
Riddle-me, Riddle-me, Ree,
Nine, ten crows round that tree.
Riddle-me, Riddle-me, Ro,
Now forty. He won't go.
Riddle-me, Riddle-me, Ree,
How deafening crows can be!
Riddle-me, Riddle-me, Ro,
The owl's still saying "No!"
Riddle-me, Riddle-me, Ree,
Did something leave the tree?

Riddle-me, Riddle-me, Ro,
You'll have to ask a crow.
Riddle-me, Riddle-me, Ree,
The crows are following he . . .
Riddle-me, Riddle-me, Ro,
Are following *him*.

I know.

A little experience with such simple poems is fine prepara-
tion for more complex verse-and-chorus patterns found in
poems by Beatrice Schenk de Regniers.

In her poem "If We Walked on Our Hands," she is really
inviting two choruses to come in again and again:

No. 1) What a mixed-up place this world would
be
No. 2) What a mixed-up
fixed-up
topsy-turvy
sit-u-a-tion.

With a little practice the two choruses will be in the mood
for a frolic. Have one person read the first four lines of each
stanza; then invite the choruses to chime in.

IF WE WALKED ON OUR HANDS

If we walked on our hands
instead of our feet
And we all ate paper
instead of meat
What a mixed-up place this world would be
What a mixed-up
fixed-up
topsy-turvy
sit-u-a-tion.

If we wore our hats
  on our behinds
And all we ate
  were melon rinds
What a mixed-up place this world would be
What a mixed-up
      fixed-up
      topsy-turvy
      sit-u-a-tion.

If babies worked
  while papas played
If the children gave orders
  and parents obeyed
What a mixed-up place this world would be
What a mixed-up
      fixed-up
      topsy-turvy
      sit-u-a-tion.

More conventional and more wistful is the old poem "White Horses" by Eleanor Farjeon. This takes us to England at a time when a horse-drawn farm wagon, or wain, was a common sight, and when a child was urged to count the white horses he saw, and on the ninth make a wish, which would surely come true.

Eleanor Farjeon puts her chorus of four lines at the beginning and end of her poem. In between she tells of seeing eight white horses . . . "But oh for the ninth one!"

Often we have practiced the four-line chorus as a group, with our voices adding to the mysterious admonition. Then, one after the other, eight children repeat the lines that tell of seeing a white horse. A ninth one can read the stanza of disappointment, "But oh for the ninth one . . ." Put it all together, and you have a gently moving experience for all.

WHITE HORSES

Count the white horses you meet on the way,
Count the white horses, child, day after day,
Keep a wish ready for wishing—if you
Wish on the ninth horse, your wish will come
    true.

I saw a white horse at the end of the lane,
I saw a white horse canter down by the shore,
I saw a white horse that was drawing a wain,
And one drinking out of a trough: that made
    four.

I saw a white horse gallop over the down,
I saw a white horse looking over a gate,
I saw a white horse on the way into town,
And one on the way coming back: that made
    eight.

But oh for the ninth one: where he tossed his
    mane,
And cantered and galloped and whinnied and
    swished
His silky white tail, I went looking in vain,
And the wish I had ready could never be
    wished.

Count the white horses you meet on the way,
Count the white horses, child, day after day,
Keep a wish ready for wishing—if you
Wish on the ninth horse, your wish will come
    true.

Eve Merriam swings boldly into today with the poem
"Tube Time." It provides the opportunity for a chorus and
several solo voices, each taking one of the rhyming couplets.

T U B E   T I M E

I turned on the TV
and what did I see?

I saw a can of cat food talking,
a tube of toothpaste walking.

> Peanuts, popcorn,
> cotton flannel.
> Jump up, jump up,
> switch the channel.

I turned to Station B
and what did I see?

I saw a shampoo bottle crying,
a pile of laundry flying.

> Peanuts, popcorn,
> cotton flannel.
> Jump up, jump up,
> switch the channel.

I turned to Station B
and what did I see?

I saw two spray cans warring,
a cup of coffee snoring.

> Peanuts, popcorn,
> cotton flannel.
> Jump up, jump up,
> switch the channel.

I turned to Station E
and what did I see?

I saw dancing fingers dialing,
an upset stomach smiling.

Peanuts, popcorn,
cotton flannelette:
jump up, jump up,
turn off the set.

David McCord gives the perfect setup for choruses in the
next poem:

BANANAS AND CREAM

Bananas and cream,
Bananas and cream:
All we could say was
Bananas and cream.

We couldn't say fruit,
We wouldn't say cow,
We didn't say sugar—
We don't say it now.

Bananas and cream,
Bananas and cream,
All we could shout was
Bananas and cream.

We didn't say why,
We didn't say how;
We forgot it was fruit,
We forgot the old cow;
We *never* said sugar,
We only said *WOW!*

Bananas and cream,
Bananas and cream;
All that we want is
Bananas and cream!

We didn't say dish,
We didn't say spoon;

We said not tomorrow,
But NOW and HOW SOON

Bananas and cream
Bananas and cream?
We yelled for bananas,
Bananas and scream!

For more fun, have a taste of "Beautiful Soup" by Lewis Carroll, which can be read with several choruses and a solo or two.

BEAUTIFUL SOUP

Beautiful Soup, so rich and green,
Waiting in a hot tureen!
Who for such dainties would not stoop?
Soup of the evening, beautiful Soup!
Soup of the evening, beautiful Soup!
    Beau-ootiful Soo-oop!
    Beau-ootiful Soo-oop!
Soo-oop of the e—e—evening,
    Beautiful, beautiful Soup!

Beautiful Soup! Who cares for fish,
Game, or any other dish?
Who would not give all else for a
Pennyworth only of beautiful Soup?
Pennyworth only of beautiful Soup?
    Beau-ootiful Soo-oop!
    Beau-ootiful Soo-oop!
Soo-oop of the e—e—evening,
    Beautiful, beauti-FUL SOUP!

A number of the poems of folk literature personify elements of nature—the wind, the thunder, the clouds—and present a vivid picture and stirring ideas. Often those poems work well with several solo voices and one or more choruses.

41

One of the most moving of these comes to us from Siberia:

P R A I S E   S O N G   O F   T H E   W I N D

Trees with weak roots
I will strike, I the wind.
I will roar, I will whistle.

Haycocks built today
I will scatter, I the wind,
I will roar, I will whistle.

Badly made haycocks
I will carry off, I the wind.
I will roar, I will whistle.

Uncovered stacks of sheaves
I will soak through, I the wind.
I will roar, I will whistle.

Houses not tightly roofed
I will destroy, I the wind.
I will roar, I will whistle.

Hay piled in sheds
I will tear apart, I the wind,
I will roar, I will whistle.

Fire kindled in the road
I will set flickering, I the wind.
I will roar, I will whistle.

Houses with bad smoke-holes
I will shake, I the wind.
I will roar, I will whistle.

The farmer who does not think
I will make to think, I the wind.
I will roar, I will whistle.

The worthless slug-a-bed
I will wake, I the wind.
I will roar, I will whistle.

I shall never forget hearing second graders present their
reading of the old Navaho folk poem beginning "The voice
that beautifies the land." By prearrangement, one small
group read the first line of each stanza; a solo voice read lines
two, three, and four; and the whole class chanted the last
two lines. Listen:

The voice that beautifies the land!
The voice above,
The voice of the thunder,
Among the dark clouds
Again and again it sounds,
The voice that beautifies the land.

The voice that beautifies the land!
The voice below,
The voice of the grasshopper,
Among the flowers and grasses
Again and again it sounds,
The voice that beautifies the land.

The children went on to chant two stanzas they had created on the pattern of the original, using the same opening
line and final pair:

The voice that beautifies the land!
The voice above
The voice of the wind
Through the grass
Again and again it sounds
The voice that beautifies the land.

The voice that beautifies the land!
The voice below
The voice of the lamb
Calling to its mother
Again and again it sounds
The voice that beautifies the land.

Poems with an Echo

Many poems—like many songs—provide for an echo that is a delight to create and to repeat. As a beginning, I often introduce two from folk literature that invite immediate participation and give immediate pleasure.

For the first one we form two echo groups: one to repeat the word "ever" and the other the word "never." Sometimes we practice five "evers" and then three "evers," then five "nevers" and three "nevers," then put the whole reading together. When children hear the story they are helping to spin out, they are delighted and invariably ask to do it again.

> If you ever ever ever ever ever
>   If you ever ever ever meet a whale
> You must never never never never never
>   You must never never never touch his tail:
>
> For if you ever ever ever ever ever
>   If you ever ever ever touch his tail,
> You will never never never never never
>   You will never never never meet another
>   whale.

The second folk poem we often use for the fun of echoing begins, "If all the seas were one sea." If the leader reads the first line, the group soon discovers the pattern and joins in on the responses or exclamation of alternate lines. It begins:

> If all the seas were one sea
>> What a great sea that would be!

and then it goes on in the same pattern—so quickly identi-
fied that even third graders can pick it up and join in:

> If all the trees were one tree
>> What a great tree that would be!
> If all the axes were one axe
>> What a great axe that would be!
>
> If all the men were one man
>> What a great man that would be!

Then comes the narrator's section with a final line for all
to shout:

> And if the great man took the great axe
>> and cut down the great tree
> And let it fall into the great sea
>> What a great SPLASH that would be!

On the first try, we are feeling our way through words and
lines that some may be unsure of. But when we try it again,
we get more excitement—more drama—into it.

Also from folk literature is this poem with a "dark, dark"
chorus, mounting suspense, and a grand finale:

> In a dark, dark wood there was a dark, dark
>> house,
> And in the dark, dark house there was a dark,
>> dark room,
> And in that dark, dark room there was a dark,
>> dark cupboard,
> And in that dark, dark cupboard there was a
>> dark, dark shelf,

And in that dark, dark shelf there was a dark,
   dark box,
And in that dark, dark box there was a GHOST!

The Pima Indians of the Central Plains give us this lovely echo song of the wind:

The wind now commences to sing;
The wind now commences to sing,
The land stretches before me,
Before me stretches away.

Wind's house now is thundering;
Wind's house now is thundering,
I go roaring over the land,
The land covered with thunder.

The Black Snake Wind came to me,
The Black Snake Wind came to me,
Came and wrapped itself around me,
Came here running with its songs.

Frequently, modern poets use the old echo technique and thus provide many opportunities for group involvement. Here are several very popular ones:

THE WINDSHIELD WIPERS' SONG

Late pretty late
Late pretty late
What held you up?
What held you up?
Rained cats and dogs
Rained cats and dogs
Car got a wash
Car got a wash

Weather says sleet
Weather says sleet
Low on gas?
Low on gas?
Look at the gauge
Look at the gauge
Yes you forgot
Yes you forgot

Get me new blades
Get me new blades
How's it inside?
How's it inside?
Can't make you out
Can't make you out
Turn me on fast
Turn me on fast

That's better faster
That's better faster
Car's on your tailgate
Car's on your tailgate
Try the brakes easy
Try the brakes easy
Guy must be crazy
Guy must be crazy
Guy must . . .

—David McCord

THE MYSTERIOUS CAT

I saw a proud, mysterious cat,
I saw a proud, mysterious cat,
Too proud to catch a mouse or rat—
Mew, mew, mew.

But catnip she would eat, and purr,
But catnip she would eat, and purr,

And goldfish she did much prefer—
Mew, mew, mew.

I saw a cat—'twas but a dream,
I saw a cat—'twas but a dream,
Who scorned the slave that brought her
  cream—
Mew, mew, mew.

Unless the slave were dressed in style,
Unless the slave were dressed in style,
And knelt before her all the while—
Mew, mew, mew.

Did you ever hear of a thing like that?
Did you ever hear of a thing like that?
Did you ever hear of a thing like that?
Oh, what a proud mysterious cat.
Oh, what a proud mysterious cat.
Oh, what a proud mysterious cat.
Mew . . . Mew . . . Mew.

—Vachel Lindsay

Question-and-Answer Poems

Question-and-answer poems have the perfect pattern for two-part reading. One person asks, the other answers. Or two small groups may do the questioning and answering. It becomes a game that all enjoy.

Many such poems have come down to us through the years as a part of folk literature. Old and young learned them by listening to others and joining in. When they gathered at a picnic or listened to a ballad singer in the village square, they were ready to take part.

These two from folk literature are just right for two solo voices:

"Hello, Bill."
"Where are you going, Bill?"
"Downtown, Bill"
"What for, Bill?"
"To pay my gas bill."
"How much, Bill?"
"A ten-dollar bill."
"So long, Bill."

The old poem "Did You Feed My Cow?" suggests many possibilities: one reader to ask questions; another to give the answers; several groups to chant the responses (the "Yes, Mam!" group, the "Corn an' hay" group; and so on). Participants will soon be dreaming up other variations.

DID YOU FEED MY COW?

Did you feed my cow?
  Yes, Mam!
Will you tell me how?
  Yes, Mam!
Oh, what did you give her?
  Corn an' hay.
Oh, what did you give her?
  Corn an' hay.

Did you milk her good?
  Yes, Mam!
Did you do like you should?
  Yes, Mam!
Oh, how did you milk her?
  Swish! Swish! Swish!
Oh, how did you milk her?
  Swish! Swish! Swish!

Did that cow die?
  Yes, Mam!

With a pain in her eye?
    Yes, Mam!
Oh, how did she die?
    Uh! Uh! Uh!
Oh, how did she die?
    Uh! Uh! Uh!

Did the buzzards come?
    Yes, Mam!
For to pick her bone?
    Yes, Mam!
Oh, how did they come?
    Flop! Flop! Flop!
Oh, how did they come?
    Flop! Flop! Flop!

A number of modern poems follow the question-and-answer pattern. Here are several that children like.

BANBURY FAIR

Where have you been,
    Miss Marjorie Keen?
To Banbury Fair
    In a carriage and pair.
And what could there be
    That was funny to see?
A dame in a wig
    A-dancing a jig.
And what did you get
    For six pennies, my pet?
A pink sugar mouse
    And a gingerbread house.

—Edith G. Millard

With young children, one of the most popular question-and-answer poems is the picture book entitled *Brown Bear,*

Brown Bear, What Do You See? by Bill Martin Jr. It begins
with a simple pattern that changes only slightly from one
animal to the next:

> Brown bear, brown bear,
> What do you see?
> > I see a red bird
> > Looking at me.
>
> Red bird, red bird
> What do you see?
> > I see a yellow duck
> > Looking at me.
>
> Yellow duck, yellow duck
> What do you see?

Then come a blue horse, a green frog, a purple cat, a white
dog, a black sheep, a goldfish, and finally a monkey who
says: "I see children looking at me."

Even very shy children are easily drawn into chanting
these questions and answers; and as familiarity grows, they
like to improvise and spin out their own. The first questioner
addresses another child, who answers and then directs the
same question to someone else. In this game each adds his
link to the chain.

With a little encouragement, children enjoy using the pattern to introduce familiar characters from Mother Goose or
favorite picture books:

> I see Humpty Dumpty
> Looking at me.
>
> I see Peter Rabbit
> Looking at me.

51

After coming under the spell of *Where the Wild Things Are* by Maurice Sendak, one group of second graders sang out these lines:

> I see a wild thing
> Looking at me.
>
> Wild thing, wild thing
> What do you see?
>
> I see Max
> Looking at me.

The poem "Where Have You Been?" by Margaret Wise Brown has everything young children like: a pattern of repetition that invites an echo, questions and answers, a variety of intriguing animals, plus rhyme throughout.

WHERE HAVE YOU BEEN?

Little Old Cat
Little Old Cat
Where have you been?
To see this and that
Said the Little Old Cat
That's where I've been.

Little Old Squirrel
Little Old Squirrel
Where have you been?
I've been out in a whirl
Said the Little Old Squirrel
That's where I've been.

Little Old Fish
Little Old Fish
Where do you swim?

Wherever I wish
Said the Little Old Fish
That's where I swim.

The pattern continues through eleven more stanzas about Little Brown Bird, Little Old Horse, Little Old Toad, Little Old Frog, Little Old Mole, Little Old Whale, Little Old Bee, Little Old Bunny, Little Old Lion, Little Old Mouse, and Little Old Rook. With a little encouragement, children will soon invent many more.

Another favorite is this untitled poem from *Father Fox's Pennyrhymes* by Clyde Watson:

How many miles to Old Norfolk
To see a magician breathe fire & smoke?
    One, two, three, four,
    Only three miles more.
How many miles to Christmas Cove
To eat of an applecake baked with clove?
    One, two, three, four,
    Only two miles more.

How many miles to Newburyport
For trinkets & sweets of every sort?
    One, two, three, four,
    Only one mile more.
How many miles to Lavender Spring
To hear a fine trumpeter play for the King?
    One, two, three, four,
    Here we are, we'll go no more.

In the next poem, middle-grade students in particular love to use a husky, rasping voice for the witch and an increasingly fearful tone for the questioner.

WITCH, WITCH

"Witch, witch, where do you fly?" . . .
"Under the clouds and over the sky."

"Witch, witch, what do you eat?" . . .
"Little black apples from Hurricane Street."

"Witch, witch, what do you drink?" . . .
"Vinegar, blacking, and good red ink."

"Witch, witch, where do you sleep?" . . .
"Up in the clouds where pillows are cheap."

—Rose Fyleman

The question-and-answer pattern has been around for a long time for humorous poems, which appeal to older children. One of their favorites is "Father William" by Lewis Carroll, a series of impertinent questions from the son to the argumentative, unforgettable father. A sample:

"You are old," said the youth, "as I mentioned
    before,
  And have grown most uncommonly fat;
Yet you turned a back somersault in at the
    door—
  Pray, what is the reason for that?"

"In my youth," said the sage, as he shook his
    gray locks,
  "I kept all my limbs supple
By use of this ointment—one shilling the box—
  Allow me to sell you a couple."

Finally questions are cut off by Father William:

"Do you think I can listen all day to such stuff?
  Be off, or I'll kick you down stairs!"

Poems for Two Voices

Paul Fleischman has two collections of poems that he calls "poems for two voices." These poems were written to be read aloud by two readers at once, one taking the left-hand part, the other the right. When both readers have lines on the same horizontal level, lines are to be read simultaneously.

This may sound too complicated for children, but middle graders are intrigued by the plan. With some practice, they come through with a captivating production.

The first of these books is *I Am Phoenix: Poems for Two Voices* (Harper, 1985). All of the poems are about birds: sparrows, mockingbirds, finches, doves, owls, and more—singing, soaring, complaining, rejoicing. The second, *Joyful Noise: Poems for Two Voices* (Harper, 1988), which won the 1989 Newbery Medal, is made up of poems about insects: honeybees, fireflies, grasshoppers, book lice, water striders, and more. Verbally the poet recreates the "Booming/boisterous/joyful noise" of insects.

Try this one from *Joyful Noise,* and I think you will want to go back for more:

GRASSHOPPERS

Sap's rising	
	Ground's warming
Grasshoppers are	Grasshoppers are
hatching out	hatching out
Autumn-laid eggs	
	splitting
Young stepping	
	into spring
Grasshoppers	Grasshoppers
hopping	hopping
high	

55

Grassjumpers	Grassjumpers
jumping	jumping
	far
Vaulting from	
leaf to leaf	
stem to stem	leaf to leaf
plant to plant	stem to stem
	Grass-
leapers	leapers
Grass-	
bounders	bounders
	Grass-
springers	springers
Grass-	
soarers	soarers
Leapfrogging	Leapfrogging
longjumping	longjumping
grasshoppers.	grasshoppers.

The Sound Effects of Poetry

In the English language many words imitate natural sounds: the *roar* of thunder, for example. The *jingle* of bells. The *hoot* of the owl. High school students learn this is called *onomatopoeia,* a word that may be too difficult for younger children to pronounce or spell. Yet they can easily hear its effect in the poems they read if they have the opportunity to produce those sounds themselves.

A wonderful introduction is Aileen Fisher's poem about the weather, which sparkles with sound words children love to imitate. One good way to begin is to parcel out the lines so that each person has a line to recite, using the sound effect that word suggests. For example, "It sings" will be read in a singing voice; "and bangs" with an appropriate bang; "and grumbles" with a grumbling voice. All join in on "CRASHES."

The last eight lines can be read as a solo, with all protesting on the final "Not Me!"

WEATHER IS FULL OF THE NICEST SOUNDS

Weather is full
of the nicest sounds:
it sings
and rustles
and pings
and pounds
and hums
and tinkles
and strums
and twangs
and whishes
and sprinkles
and splishes
and bangs
and mumbles
and grumbles
and rumbles
and flashes
and CRASHES.

I wonder
if thunder
frightens a bee,
a mouse in her house,
a bird in a tree,
a bear
or a hare
or a fish in the sea?
Not *me*!

Here's another favorite:

TWO CATS

Two cats were sitting in a tree,
kritte vitte vit bom bom,
a cat called Lew,
a cat called Lee,
kritte vitte vit bom bom.
"Now follow me,"
said Lew to Lee,
kritte vitte vitte vitte vit bom bom,
"for I no longer like this tree,"
kritte vitte vit bom bom!

So Lew and Lee
climbed down the tree,
kritte vitte vit bom bom.
Once down the tree
to Lew said Lee,
kritte vitte vit bom bom,
"Oh, Lew, I rather liked that tree!"
kritte vitte vitte vit bom bom.
So Lew and Lee climbed up the tree,
Kritte vitte vit bom bom!

—Danish Nursery Rhyme
Translated by N. M. Bodecker

Often children enjoy creating sound effects for a poem while someone reads the words. "Song of the Train" by David McCord is a wonderful choice for this. Clicking pencils and rulers can accompany the "Click-ety-clack" of the poem, growing faster as the words suggest or fading in the distance as the train goes by.

SONG OF THE TRAIN

Clickety-clack,
Wheels on the track,
This is the way
They begin the attack:
Click-ety-clack,
Click-ety-clack,
Click-ety, *clack*-ety,
Click-ety
Clack.

Clickety-clack,
Over the crack,
Faster and faster
The song of the track:
Clickety-clack,
Clickety-clack,
Clickety, clackety,
Clackety
Clack.

Riding in front,
Riding in back,
Everyone hears
The song of the track:
Clickety-clack,
Clickety-clack,
Clickety, *clickety*,
Clackety
Clack.

Another David McCord favorite is:

THE PICKETY FENCE

The pickety fence
The pickety fence

Give it a lick it's
The pickety fence
Give it a lick it's
A clickety fence
Give it a lick it's
A lickety fence
Give it a lick
Give it a lick
Give it a lick
With a rickety stick
Pickety
Pickety
Pickety
Pick.

It is fun to have several soloists read the poem, with a chorus coming in on "Give it a lick/Give it a lick/Give it a lick." Or the final "Pickety/Pickety/Pickety/Pick" can grow fainter, as though a child and his clicking stick are moving into the distance. And, of course, children love to do the background accompaniment with pencils and rulers going "pickety, clickety, lickety, rickety" while others chant the words. By the third or fourth go-round, you have quite a production.

For "The Washing Machine" by Jeffrey Davies, there are always eager volunteers to produce such sounds as "fwunkety" and "shlunkety."

THE WASHING MACHINE

It goes fwunkety,
    then shlunkety,
as the washing goes around.

The water spluncheses
    And it shluncheses,
as the washing goes around.

As you pick it out it splocheses,
    then it flocheses,
as the washing goes around.

But at the end it schlopperies,
    and then flopperies,
and the washing stops going round.

The Game of Rhyming Words

A poem does not have to rhyme, of course, but many children's poems have what is called "end rhyme." That is, the final word in one line repeats the sound of the final word in another, as in these lines from Mother Goose:

Higgledy, piggledy pop!
The dog ran away with the mop.

In a way, repeating the sound through rhyme is like repeating the note in a song at regular intervals. When rhyming words are a bit incongruous, rhyme adds to the humor as well.

An effective way to help children appreciate good rhyme is to make a game of having them supply the rhyming word for a poem read aloud. Read the first couplet aloud and note the rhyme of the final words in these lines. Then read the second couplet, pausing before the last word so that children can supply a word that is appropriate.

Eve Merriam's "Catch a Little Rhyme" makes a good starter.

CATCH A LITTLE RHYME

Once upon a time
I caught a little rhyme

61

I set it on the floor
but it ran right out the door

I chased it on my bicycle
but it melted to an icicle

I scooped it up in my hat
but it turned into a cat

I caught it by the tail
But it stretched into a whale

I followed it in a boat
but it changed into a goat

When I fed it tin and paper
it became a tall skyscraper

Then it grew into a kite
and flew far out of sight . . .

For somewhat older children, this dramatic bit from folk literature is always fun:

"Fire! Fire!"
Cried Mrs. McGuire.
"Where! Where!"
Cried Mrs. Blair.
"All over town!"
Cried Mrs. Brown.
"We'd better jump!"
Cried Mrs. Gump.
"That would be silly!"
Cried Mrs. Brunelli.
"It looks too risky!"
Cried Mrs. Matruski.
"What'll we do?"
Cried Mrs. LaRue.
"Turn in the alarm!"

Cried Mrs. Storm.
"Save us! Save us!"
Cried Mrs. Davis.
The fire department got the call
And the firemen saved them one and all.

Then try these from David McCord:

J A M B O R E E

A rhyme for ham? *Jam.*
A rhyme for mustard? *Custard.*
A rhyme for steak? *Cake.*
A rhyme for rice? *Another slice.*
A rhyme for stew? *You.*
A rhyme for mush? *Hush.*
A rhyme for prunes? *Goons.*
A rhyme for pie? *I.*
A rhyme for tea? *Me.*
For the pantry shelf? *Myself.*

I   W A N T   Y O U   T O   M E E T . . .

. . . Meet Ladybug,
her little sister Sadiebug,
her mother, Mrs. Gradybug,
her aunt, that nice oldmaidybug,
and Baby—she's a fraidybug.

Thus children are experiencing the changing moods of poetry—from the quiet whisper of "Old Snake Has Gone to Sleep" to the topsy-turvy humor of "If We Walked on Our Hands." They feel the change in the rhythm, too, from the back and forth of David McCord's windshield wipers to the "clickety-clack" of his train. They become aware of the mar-

63

velous range of poetic sounds because they have helped to produce the "fwunkety," "shlunkety" of Jeffrey Davies's washing machine.

As poetry becomes a part of them, they are ready for more.

3   *Moving into Poetry*

EVEN SMALL children come under the spell of rhythmical language and song. And at an early age they respond by waving arms or legs in time to the "Pat-a-cake, Pat-a-cake" of Mother Goose, or rattling the side of the crib to the beat of a recording.

A two-year-old sways to the rhythmical tick-tock of the grandfather's clock. Five- and six-year-olds play singing games and move as the words of the song direct. Seven-year-olds use pencils and rulers to produce sound effects for the "clickety-clack" of David McCord's "Song of the Train" and then crawl across the floor to represent a string of boxcars gaining speed. Middle graders and teenagers will swing and sway, clap and tap, to the sense and sound of song or poem. For all ages, body movement becomes one of the most effective ways of adding to pleasure in poetry.

Singing Games Make a Good Beginning

One of the simplest singing games can be used with just one child or with a group. It begins:

> If you're happy and you know it,
> Clap your hands (*clap, clap*)
> If you're happy and you know it,
> Clap your hands (*clap, clap*)
>
> If you're happy and you know it,
> Your face will surely show it.
> If you're happy and you know it,
> Clap your hands (*clap, clap*).

The song is so old that there are many variations, and the pattern is so simple that more and more stanzas can be added.

For example:

> If you're angry and you know it,
> Stamp your feet (*stamp, stamp*)
> If you're sad and you know it,
> Shed a tear (*sniff, sniff*)
>
> If you're joyous and you know it,
> Jump for joy (*jump, jump*).

Participants will soon note that the tempo changes with the mood: quick and light for "happy," soft and slow for "sad," stronger and bolder for "angry." Gradually they build head-to-foot understanding of the harmony between rhythm and meaning.

Another favorite that can be used with one child or with a small circle begins with the chorus.

> Here we go Looby-loo
> Here we go Looby-light
> Here we go Looby-loo
> All on a Saturday night.

Players follow the directions as they sing each stanza.

> I put my right hand in
> I take my right hand out
> I give my right hand a shake, shake, shake
> And turn myself about.

Chorus

> I put my left hand in
> I take my left hand out
> I give my left hand a shake, shake, shake
> And turn myself about.

Chorus

> I put my right foot in
> I take my right foot out
> I give my right foot a shake, shake, shake
> And turn myself about.

Chorus

> I put my left foot in
> I take my left foot out
> I give my left foot a shake, shake, shake
> And turn myself about.

Chorus

> I put my whole self in
> I take my whole self out

I give myself a shake, shake, shake
And turn myself about.

Chorus

In *The Fireside Book of Children's Songs,* Marie Winn gives music and words to "The Hokey Pokey," a singing game that is surely a first cousin of "Looby-loo." The final directions in each stanza add more fun to the game:

And then you do the hokey-pokey
And turn yourself about,
And that's what it's all about! Hey!

A splendid collection of songs suggesting movement is *Eye Winker, Tom Tinker, Chin Chopper: Fifty Musical Fingerplays with Piano Arrangements and Guitar Chords* by Tom Glazer (Doubleday, 1973). Many of these can be extended easily beyond fingerplay to complete body movement. Children revel in these singing games. All the while, they are becoming more deeply aware of rhythm.

Jump-Rope Jingles Add to the Fun

Whether your children are rope-jumpers or not, they will enjoy chanting the words and following the directions of some of the traditional jump-rope jingles.

Teddy Bear, Teddy Bear, turn around,
Teddy Bear, Teddy Bear, touch the ground.

Teddy Bear, Teddy Bear, read the news,
Teddy Bear, Teddy Bear, shine your shoes.

Teddy Bear, Teddy Bear, go upstairs,
Teddy Bear, Teddy Bear, say your prayers.

Teddy Bear, Teddy Bear, turn out the light,
Teddy Bear, Teddy Bear, say GOOD NIGHT!

Another favorite that immediately suggests body movement is:

Spanish dancer, do the split, split, split,
Spanish dancer, do the kick, kick, kick,
Spanish dancer, turn around, round, round,
Spanish dancer, touch the ground, ground,
　　ground.

One old version substitutes these two final lines:

Spanish dancer, do the kangaroo,
Spanish dancer, out skidoo!

Any variation is possible so long as it adds to the meaning and fits the rhythm of the chant. Participants like to come up with their own improvisations.

"Charlie Chaplin went to France" is a jump-rope jingle that came out of the World War I period. The first three lines give the introduction:

Charlie Chaplin went to France
To teach the ladies how to dance,
And this is how he taught them:

Heel, toe, over you go.
Heel, toe, over you go.
Salute to the captain,
And bow to the queen,
And turn your back
On the submarine!

Time for a Warm-up

The simple movements for a singing game such as "Here we go Looby-loo" seem to come easily for any child or group. Perhaps this is because the directions are quite literal: "I put my right foot in/I take my right foot out." Even this simple kind of movement gives pleasure and pride in participation. However, to become involved in real poetry, they must move with imagination and feeling as well.

Often a warm-up period with background music helps us become aware of ways we can use our bodies to express feelings and ideas. As a beginning, I ask each to find his or her space on the floor; that is, space to stretch arms to the side, back, and front without taking up someone else's space.

Then we begin to explore the ways we can use our hands (at first in tight fists, then with fingers outspread, or flapping from the wrists); our shoulders (rising and falling, rotating backward, then forward); our heads (up and down, rotating, drooping, held high); our knees (flexed slightly, or in a deep bend); one leg and then the other (slowly lifted forward, then swinging around to the back); and so on.

But how do we use these remarkable parts of our body machine to express ideas and feeling? Children will have fun trying out various assignments: Walk with confidence. Tiptoe stealthily. Walk flatfoot like a clown. Walk like a sad old man. Imagine you are picking up a heavy sack of apples and carry it on your shoulder. Hop like a sparrow. Swim like a fish. Fly like a bird. Move like a robot.

And with our faces: Look sad, then tired. Happy, then angry. Mischievous, then troubled.

Then we try out the shapes our bodies can assume: tall and slim with arms reaching to the sky, leaning to one side and then the other, leaning forward to touch the floor like an inverted U, curling up on the floor like a cat.

Then with music to egg us on, we try skipping, then leaping, and swinging and swaying, then winding down to slow motion.

At some point it is fun to have each child select a partner, one to make the initial movements, the other to mirror these movements, always in time to the music, always in pairs, but not touching. That takes more control and concentration. Soon partners become absorbed in the effort to move with expression and meaning.

Move as the Poet Directs

As children experiment with different movements, inhibitions seem to disappear. Even the shy ones will be drawn in.

At this stage I like to read aloud a poem that names specific movements: hopping, skipping, swaying, for example. Sometimes we practice such movements before the poem is read. Or I may read the poem and ask children to listen for words that suggest how they might move, then try skipping or hopping.

Now we listen to the poem again, perhaps tapping out the rhythm with our feet. Or we walk to the rhythm, interrupting our walk to skip or hop as the lines may suggest.

When the poem is read again, we put it all together: hopping, skipping, slowing down to listen, sometimes using our faces to reflect the mood.

These poems make good starters:

BEDTIME

Hop away
Skip away
Jump away
Leap!
Day is all crumpled
And lies in a heap.

Jump away
Skip away
Hop away
Creep!
Night comes and coaxes
The world to sleep.

—Patricia Hubbell

I CAN FLY

I can fly, of course,
Very low,
Not fast,
Rather slow.
I spread my arms
Like wings,
Lean on the wind,
And my body zings
About.
Nothing showy—
A few loops
And turns—
But for the most
Part,
I just coast.

However,
Since people are prone
To talk about
It,
I generally prefer,
Unless I am alone,
just to walk about.

—Felice Holman

An excerpt from **A DANCE**

Heel, toe,
Heel, toe,
Curtsy and caper
And over you go.
Toe, heel,
Toe, heel,
The tin trumpets toot
And the violins squeal.
The melody mounts
From a reel to a roar,
We sweep 'cross the carpet
And crash to the floor.

—Karla Kuskin

The next poem is taken from *Songs of the Dream People,* edited and illustrated by James Houston, a collection of chants and images from the Indians and Eskimos of North America. This poem comes from Eskimos who live in central Canada north of the Arctic Circle.

My arms, they wave high in the air,
My hands, they flutter behind my back,
They wave above my head
Like the wings of a bird.
Let me move my feet.
Let me dance.
Let me shrug my shoulders
Let me shake my body.
Let me crouch down.
My arms, let me fold them.
Let me hold my hands under my chin.

When students in the Poetry Workshop at Lehigh University introduced us to this Eskimo poem, they asked us to make a circle, all facing the center. While the poem was being read in a slow chant, we moved as the lines directed: arms waving, then hands fluttering, and so on. Finally we crouched on our knees, folding our arms and holding our hands under our chins. I had the feeling I was participating in an ancient pageant that had enveloped me.

With the next folk poem, "Dance of the Animals," I often suggest that children divide into four groups: one for each of the three stanzas and one to chant the repeated final line, which becomes the chorus. As the poem is read and the chorus chanted, one group follows the directions in the first stanza about the fish; the second, those in the stanza about the bird; and the third takes over the final stanza about the monkey. The resulting performance will be one to remember.

DANCE OF THE ANIMALS

I throw myself to the left,
I turn myself to the right,
I am the fish
Who glides through the water, who glides,
Who twists himself, who leaps.
Everything lives, everything dances, everything
   sings.

The bird flies,
Flies, flies, flies,
Goes, comes back, passes,
Mounts, hovers, and drops down.
I am the bird.
Everything lives, everything dances, everything
   sings.

The monkey, from bough to bough,
Runs, leaps, and jumps,
With his wife, with his little one,

74

His mouth full, his tail in the air:
This is the monkey, this is the monkey.
Everything lives, everything dances, everything
    sings.

—Pygmy (Africa)

Move to Interpret the Poet's Lines

Frequently the poet only suggests an idea, leaving the reader or listener to interpret the mood and meaning for himself. Often rhythm is the key to meaning. The person who moves to the melody of the lines as they are read aloud may get a deeper understanding of the poem than one who sits on the sidelines. Involvement through body movement seems to help stretch the imagination and broaden understanding.

A poem I like to use at this stage is "The Prayer of the Ox" by Carmen Bernos de Gasztold. It is one of twenty-seven poems in her collection entitled *Prayers from the Ark,* published originally in French and translated into English by Rumer Godden. The first poem is "Noah's Prayer," beginning "Lord,/what a menagerie!" Each of the others is the prayer of one of the animals on Noah's Ark: the Old Horse, the Cat, the Rooster, the Giraffe, the Little Ducks, and so on.

Not many children I meet have ever seen an ox, even a picture of one. They know it is a beast of burden, heavy and plodding, but that is all. But once they have moved to the rhythm of the poem, they feel close to the weary creature.

I like to read this poem at the slow, heavy pace of the ox and ask children to move as the poet suggests. Soon I see shoulders begin to sag and heads droop. As children pace their steps to the accent of the lines, they understand the complaint of the ox. His prayer seems to become their own.

THE PRAYER OF THE OX

Dear God, give me time.
Men are always so driven!
Make them understand that I can never hurry.
Give me time to eat.
Give me time to plod.
Give me time to sleep.
Give me time to think.

Amen

For a complete contrast, we often turn to "The Prayer of the Butterfly," also from *Prayers from the Ark*. Think of the butterfly you have watched over a flower bed: flitting from blossom to blossom, now rising a bit, then down, back and over, hovering, then into a tiny soar, off to another blossom, teetering on the edge of a petal, and off again.

THE PRAYER OF THE BUTTERFLY

Lord!
Where was I?
Oh, yes! This flower, this sun,
thank You! Your world is beautiful!
This scent of roses . . .
Where was I?
A drop of dew
rolls to sparkle in a lily's heart.
I have to go . . .
Where? I do not know!
The wind has painted fancies
on my wings.
Fancies . . .
Where was I?

Oh, yes! Lord,
I had something to tell you:

Amen

As you read the poem aloud, you will find yourself pausing, hovering, exclaiming, flitting from comment to query.
And as you move with the children, I think you will have a
new sense of the fluttering dance of the butterfly. The poet
never uses such words as dance, flutter, flitter, up, down,
lightly, tripping. It is the rhythm of her language that suggests this kind of movement. Those of us who have moved to
the rhythm of "The Prayer of the Butterfly" can feel it in
every muscle. Children respond eagerly.

Suppose the poem is about machines. How can we move
to suggest the heavy grinding motion of machines? The jerky
up-and-down of diggers and pumps? The pushing and scrap-
ing and dumping of road builders?

As the next poem is read aloud, invite children to act out
the lines.

A TIME FOR BUILDING

A dozen machines
come roaring down,
tractors and shovels,
hydraulics and dumps,
mixers and graders,
diggers and pumps,

pushing and groaning and moving the road
to another place in town.

—Myra Cohn Livingston

Eve Merriam's poem "Bam, Bam, Bam" closes in on an
even more dramatic scene, where houses, stores, walls, and
chimneys are being demolished to make way for "a building/
With forty-seven floors." Workmen with their pickaxes are

77

part of it, but the steel wrecking-ball is the protagonist, "changing it all."

BAM, BAM, BAM

Pickaxes, pickaxes swinging today,
Plaster clouds flying every which way.

Workmen are covered with white dust like
    snow,
Oh, come see the great demolition show!

Slam, slam, slam,
Goes the steel wrecking-ball;
Bam, bam, bam,
Against a stone wall.

It's raining bricks and wood
In my neighborhood.
Down go the houses,
Down go the stores,
Up goes a building
With forty-seven floors.

Crash goes a chimney,
Pow goes a hall,
Zowie goes a doorway,
Zam goes a wall.

Slam, slam, slam,
Goes the steel wrecking-ball;
Bam, bam, bam,
Changing it all.

The rhythm of "the great demolition show" is not the music children find in many poems, but it is the rhythm urban children hear in the street. These are sounds all children seem to find fascinating.

They are quick to move to the swing of the pickaxes, to the

"bam, bam, bam" of the wrecking-ball, to go down as houses and stores go down, and to create the sounds the poet spells out so vividly.

"Bam, Bam, Bam" can be performed by several groups: the workmen with pickaxes, the steel wrecking-ball, houses and stores about to topple and then crash, and so on. Also, it is a poem that sparks discussion about urban demolition—its uses and abuses. It can become an invitation to children to talk about their neighborhoods and the changes they see taking place.

Body Movement Leads to Dance

One summer a second-grade teacher, who had been a Martha Graham student, enrolled in our Poetry Workshop and gave us new appreciation of dance as a way of understanding and enjoying poetry.

For her demonstration she wore a black leotard and danced, without music, as someone read these four poems selected from a collection written by city children about the city.

THE LONESOME BOY

The hungry child roams the streets alone
He goes about and wishes he were home
He sits on a rock and cries, "Why do they let
  me die?"
He walks the streets with a sorrowful heart
He feels as if he is torn apart.

—Vicky White

WHO AM I?

I walk through crowded streets
Dirt and broken glass beneath my feet.

I gaze up at the crying red sky
And ask, "Who am I?"

—Stella Mancillas

M E

mean, hating
Running, talking, falling
Not liking anyone
Sad

—Danny

NO CHAINS

Look!
No chains on my arms
No chains on my legs
No chains on them
Can't you see?
But the chains on my mind are keeping
me from being FREE!

—Howard Jones

As the dancer was about to begin, three children happened to come to the doorway. On the spur of the moment she asked if they would like to help. Wide-eyed, they agreed. She posted them at various spots on the open floor, which she explained would represent a city street. They would make the motions of walking without moving from the same spot. She would dance among them, she told them, as though going down the street, where people were walking along.

Then the reading began. The dancer moved in and out among the pedestrians, her movements and facial expression interpreting the language of the poems.

The simple poems of four city children were the inspiration, but her dance made their poems sing out to everyone in that group.

Many poems lend themselves to interpretive dance. Here are two poems children love:

JUBA DANCE

Juba jump and Juba sing,
Juba cut dat pigeon's wing!
Juba kick off Juba's shoe,
Juba dance dat Juba do!
Juba whirl dat foot about,
Juba blow dat candle out!
Juba circle, raise de latch,
Juba do dat Long Dog Scratch!

—Creole Folk Song

Who will, who will,
play this game,
play this game,
jump in the air
jump in the air,
tremble in the knees,
jump in the air,
blow up in the air?
Ayii, Ayii.

—Eastern Eskimos

Ivy Eastwick's poem "Shadow Dance" is a good one for two children to interpret—one the dancer and the other "Shadow," to mirror the movements of the first.

SHADOW DANCE

O Shadow,
Dear Shadow,
Come, Shadow,
And dance!

81

On the wall
In the firelight
Let both of
Us prance!
I raise my
Arms, thus!
And you raise
Your arms, so!
And dancing
And leaping
And laughing
We go!
From the wall
To the ceiling
From ceiling
To wall.
Just you and
I, Shadow,
And none else
At all.

It seems to take more imagination and a more inventive spirit to dance to poems that tell, not of people moving, but of the wind curling and whirling or the "night coming softly and slowly." Yet children who have moved like a butterfly or an ox, who have clacked along like a railroad train, or jumped to the rhythm of an Eskimo dance, are ready to let their feelings take over and experiment. They seem to know intuitively how to curl and whirl, to move softly, or to "amble, ramble, scramble" with feeling.

Some children may wish to dance alone or to dance with a partner. Or they may decide to divide the poem into segments, each to be interpreted by a different group.

Sometimes they like to create background sound effects: the wind "running over the sand," for example, or the howl and growl, the yip and yap, of dogs in the full of the moon.

The following poems are among those that children dance to with great interest and satisfaction.

NIGHT

The night is coming softly, slowly;
Look, it's getting hard to see.
    Through the windows,
    Through the door,
    Pussyfooting
    On the floor,
    Dragging shadows,
    Crawling,
    Creeping,
    Soon it will be time for sleeping.
Pull down the shades.
Turn on the light.
Let's pretend it isn't night.
          —Mary Ann Hoberman

THE WIND CAME RUNNING

The Wind came running
over the sand,
it caught and held me
by the hand.

It curled and whirled
and danced with me
down to the edge
of the dashing sea.

We danced together,
the Wind and I,
to the cry of a gull
and a wild sea cry.

          —Ivy O. Eastwick

FULL OF THE MOON

It's full of the moon
The dogs dance out
Through brush and bush and bramble.
They howl and yowl
And growl and prowl.
They amble, ramble, scramble.
They rush through brush.
They push through bush.
They yip and yap and hurr.
They lark around and bark around
With prickles on their fur.
They two-step in the meadow.
They polka on the lawn.
Tonight's the night
The dogs dance out
And chase their tails till dawn.

—Karla Kuskin

Impromptu dance inspired by poetry read aloud is great fun. As children tiptoe or swirl or "pussyfoot" across the floor, or become dogs who "chase their tails till dawn," poetry comes alive.

4 Poetry for Pantomime and Drama

MANY POEMS lend themselves beautifully to play-acting, either with or without words spoken by the performers. And nothing seems to make a poem so real to young people as playing the dramatic parts suggested by verses read aloud.

Those who have tried skipping, running, and flying as a poet suggests are already into pantomime. Often this is movement by just one performer unrelated to the movements of others. When two or more are interacting, the dramatic elements seem sharper, and the experience becomes more memorable.

The simplest kind of playacting is pantomime, since there are no speaking parts. Sometimes children like to add sound effects. When they become involved, they may reach for improvised properties and even bits and pieces of costumes. They readily let imagination take over and move into the action of the poem.

Poems That Invite Pantomime

For the youngest, there are many Mother Goose rhymes that inspire pantomime: Jack and Jill; Little Miss Muffet (and her spider); Mistress Mary (and her "pretty maids all in a row"); Little Jack Horner; Tom, Tom the piper's son; and many more. Since all of these are songs, it is fun to have one group of children singing the words, while others act out the tiny tale.

Christina Rossetti's "Mix a Pancake" is perfect for pantomime because it is explicit:

MIX A PANCAKE

Mix a pancake,
Stir a pancake,
  Pop it in a pan;
Fry a pancake,
Toss the pancake—
  Catch it if you can.

Sitting on the floor, as though at the beach, children love to act out "Sitting in the Sand" by Karla Kuskin.

Sitting in the sand and the sea comes up
So you put your hands together
And you use them like a cup
And you dip them in the water
With a scooping sort of motion
And before the sea goes out again
You have a sip of ocean.

In snowball season, this one gives great pleasure too:

READ THIS WITH GESTURES

It isn't proper, I guess you know,
  To dip your hands—like this—in the snow,

And make a snowball, and look for a hat,
And try to knock it off—like that!

—John Ciardi

Another favorite for pantomime:

THE HUNTSMEN

Three jolly gentlemen,
  In coats of red,
Rode their horses
  Up to bed.

Three jolly gentlemen
  Snored till morn,
Their horses chomping
  The golden corn.

Three jolly gentlemen,
  At break of day,
Came clitter-clatter down the stairs
  And galloped away.

—Walter de la Mare

Broomsticks make good "horses" for the "three jolly gentlemen." Although this poem has no dialogue, it provides opportunity for great sound effects for the snoring huntsmen and chomping horses.

Shel Silverstein's "Boa Constrictor" suggests dramatic action by the boa constrictor and his victim as the poem is read aloud. Threatening tones and appropriate hissing and groaning add to the effect.

BOA CONSTRICTOR

Oh, I'm being eaten
By a boa constrictor,

A boa constrictor,
A boa constrictor,
I'm being eaten by a boa constrictor,
And I don't like it—one bit.
Well, what do you know?
It's nibblin' my toe.
Oh, gee,
It's up to my knee.
Oh, my,
It's up to my thigh.
Oh, fiddle,
It's up to my middle.
Oh, heck,
It's up to my neck.
Oh, dread,
It's upmmmmmmmmmmfffffffff . . .

A very different poem, also without dialogue, can become the basis for an impressive bit of pageantry with two or more children participating. "Song of the Sun and Moon" comes from the Navaho Indians.

SONG OF THE SUN AND MOON

The first man holds it in his hands,
He holds the sun in his hands.
In the center of the sky, he holds it in his
    hands.
As he holds it in his hands, it starts upward.

The first woman holds it in her hands,
She holds the moon in her hands.
In the center of the sky, she holds it in her
    hands.
As she holds it in her hands, it starts upward.

The first man holds it in his hands,
He holds the sun in his hands.
In the center of the sky, he holds it in his
hands.
As he holds it in his hands, it starts
downward.

The first woman holds it in her hands,
She holds the moon in her hands.
In the center of the sky, she holds it in her
hands.
As she holds it in her hands, it starts
downward.

One child or group can represent "the first man"; a second child or group can represent "the first woman." As the first stanza is read, "the first man" (or the group representing "the first man") will move as the poem directs. As these players hold the sun in place, the second stanza directs "the first woman" (or the group representing her) to lift the moon to the center of the sky. With the moon in place, "the first man" brings the sun downward and so on.

As the two groups face each other, the simple language and the movement it suggests create the mood of a primitive ritual, which indeed it may have been at one time.

Poems with Speaking Parts

Much as children enjoy pantomiming a poem, they are even more delighted when it includes speaking parts for a mini-drama. For very young children, Mother Goose provides just the right opportunity in "There were three little kittens" and "Six little mice sat down to spin."

There were three little kittens
Put on their mittens
To eat some Christmas pie.
Mew, mew, mew, mew,
Mew, mew, mew.

These three little kittens
They lost their mittens,
And all began to cry.
Mew, mew, mew, mew,
Mew, mew, mew.

Go, go, naughty kittens,
And find your mittens,
Or you shan't have any pie.
Mew, mew, mew, mew,
Mew, mew, mew.

These three little kittens
They found their mittens,
And joyfully they did cry:
Mew, mew, mew, mew,
Mew, mew, mew.

O Granny, dear!
Our mittens are here,
Make haste and cut up the pie!
Purr-rr, purr-rr,
Purr-rr-rr.

Six little mice sat down to spin;
Pussy passed by and she peeped in.
What are you doing, my little men?
Weaving coats for gentlemen.
Shall I come in and cut off your threads?
No, no, Mistress Pussy, you'd bite off our heads.
Oh, no, I'll not; I'll help you to spin.
That may be so, but you don't come in.

The next nine poems can become intriguing mini-dramas to act out. They range from the very old to the very new, and in subject matter from fantasy to high tech, from the bedtime argument between child and parents to the small boasting of seven pool players who have left school.

MRS. SNIPKIN AND MRS. WOBBLECHIN

Skinny Mrs. Snipkin,
With her little pipkin,*
Sat by the fireside a-warming of her toes.
Fat Mrs. Wobblechin,
With her little doublechin,
Sat by the window a-cooling of her nose.

Says this one to that one,
"Oh! you silly fat one,
Will you shut the window down? You're
freezing me to death!"
Says that one to t'other one,
"Good gracious, how you bother one!
There isn't air enough for me to draw my
precious breath!"

Skinny Mrs. Snipkin,
Took her little pipkin,
Threw it straight across the room as hard as
she could throw;
Hit Mrs. Wobblechin
On her little doublechin,
And out of the window a-tumble she did go.

—Laura E. Richards

* A small earthen pot.

91

THE FLATTERED FLYING FISH

Said the shark to the Flying Fish over the
    phone:
"Will you join me tonight? I am dining alone.
Let me order a nice little dinner for two!
And come as you are, in your shimmering
    blue."

Said the Flying Fish: "Fancy remembering me,
And the dress that I wore to the Porpoises'
    tea!"
"How could I forget?" said the Shark in his
    guile:
"I expect you at eight!" and rang off with a
    smile.

She has powdered her nose; she has put on
    her things;
She is off with one flap of her luminous wings.
O little one, lovely, light-hearted and vain,
The Moon will not shine on your beauty again!
                     —E. V. Rieu

LITTLE JOHN BOTTLEJOHN

Little John Bottlejohn lived on a hill,
    And a blithe little man was he.
He won the heart of a pretty mermaid
    Who lived in the deep blue sea.
And every evening she used to sit
    And sing by the rocks of the sea!
"Oh! little John Bottlejohn, pretty John
      Bottlejohn,
    Won't you come out to me?"

Little John Bottlejohn heard her song,
    And he opened his little door,

And he hopped and he skipped, and he
    skipped and he hopped,
      Until he came down to the shore.
And there on the rocks sat the little mermaid,
    And still she was singing so free,
"Oh! little John Bottlejohn, pretty John
    Bottlejohn,
      Won't you come out to me?"

Little John Bottlejohn made a bow,
    And the mermaid, she made one too;
And she said, "Oh! I never saw anyone half
    So perfectly sweet as you!
In my lovely home 'neath the ocean foam,
    How happy we both might be!
Oh! little John Bottlejohn, pretty John
    Bottlejohn,
      Won't you come down with me?"

Little John Bottlejohn said, "Oh yes!
    I'll willingly go with you
And I never shall quail at the sight of your tail,
    For perhaps I may grow one, too."
So he took her hand, and he left the land,
    And plunged in the foaming main.
And little John Bottlejohn, pretty John
    Bottlejohn,
      Never was seen again.

            —Laura E. Richards

THE OLD WIFE AND THE GHOST

There was an old wife and she lived all alone
    In a cottage not far from Hitchin:
And one bright night, by the full moon light,
    Comes a ghost right into her kitchen.

About that kitchen neat and clean
　　The ghost goes puttering round.
But the poor old wife is deaf as a boot
　　And so hears never a sound.

The ghost blows up the kitchen fire,
　　As bold as bold can be;
He helps himself from the larder shelf,
　　But never a sound hears she.

He blows on his hands to make them warm,
　　And whistles aloud "Whee-hee!"
But still as a sack the old soul lies
　　And never a sound hears she.

From corner to corner he runs about,
　　And into the cupboard he peeps;
He rattles the door and bumps the floor,
　　But still the old wife sleeps.

Jangle and bang go the pots and pans,
　　As he throws them all around;
And the plates and mugs and dishes and jugs,
　　He flings them all to the ground.

Madly the ghost tears up and down
　　And screams like a storm at sea;
And at last the old wife stirs in her bed—
　　And it's "Drat those mice," says she.

Then the first cock crows and morning shows
　　And the troublesome ghost's away.
But oh! what a pickle the poor wife sees
　　When she gets up next day.

"Them's tidy big mice," the old wife thinks,
　　And off she goes to Hitchin,
And a tidy big cat she fetches back
　　To keep the mice from her kitchen.

　　　　　　　　　　　　—James Reeves

GET UP AND BAR THE DOOR

It fell about the Martinmas time,
　　And a gay time it was then,
When our goodwife got puddings to make,
　　And she's boiled them in the pan.

The wind so cold blew south and north,
　　And blew into the floor;
Quoth our goodman to our goodwife,
　　"Get up and bar the door."

"My hand is in my household work,
　　Goodman, as ye may see;
And it will not be barred for a hundred years,
　　If it's to be barred by me!"

They made a pact between them both,
　　They made it firm and sure,
That whosoe'er should speak the first,
　　Should rise and bar the door.

Then by there came two gentlemen,
　　At twelve o'clock at night,
And they could see neither house nor hall,
　　Nor coal nor candlelight.

"Now whether is this a rich man's house
　　Or whether is it a poor?"
But never a word would one of them speak,
　　For barring of the door.

The guests they ate the white puddings,
　　And then they ate the black;
Tho' much the goodwife thought to herself,
　　Yet never a word she spake.

Then said one stranger to the other,
　　"Here, man, take ye my knife;

Do ye take off the old man's beard,
  And I'll kiss the goodwife."

"There's no hot water to scrape it off,
  And what shall we do then?"
"Then why not use the pudding broth,
  That boils into the pan?"

O up then started our goodman,
  An angry man was he;
"Will ye kiss my wife before my eyes!
  And with pudding broth scald me!"

Then up and started our goodwife,
  Gave three skips on the floor;
"Goodman, you've spoken the very first word!
  Get up and bar the door!"

                  —Folk Literature

CONVERSATION

"Mother, may I stay up tonight?"
"No, dear."
"Oh dear! (She always says, 'No, dear').
But Father said I might."
"No, dear."
"He did, that is, if you thought it right."
"No, dear, it isn't right."
"Oh dear! Can I keep on the light?"
"No, dear. In spite
Of what your Father said,
You go to bed,
And in the morning you'll be bright
And glad instead
For one more day ahead."
"I might,
But not for one more night."
"No, dear—*no,* dear."

"At least I've been polite, I guess."
"Yes, dear, you've been polite—
Good night."
"Oh dear,
I'd rather stay down here—
I'm quite . . ."
"No, dear. Now, out of sight."
("Well that was pretty near—")
"*Good* night."
("—all right.")
"Good *night*!"

—David McCord

WE REAL COOL

The Pool Players.
Seven at the Golden Shovel.

We real cool. We
Left school. We

Lurk late. We
Strike straight. We

Sing sin. We
Thin gin. We

Jazz June. We
Die soon.

—Gwendolyn Brooks

These poems provide speaking parts for only a few players. The next one can become the script for a dozen or more
voices from machines across the country, even around the
world. Children love to imitate the recorded telephone message they have sometimes heard: "I'm sorry, that number has
been disconnected." This is a poem that middle graders like
to ham up.

NANCY LARRICK

I'M SORRY SAYS THE MACHINE

I'm sorry says the machine,
Thank you for waiting says the tape recording,
Trying to connect you says the voice in the
    vacuum at the end of the line.

I'm sorry that sister is not in working order.
Please verify your brother and try him again.
I'm sorry that mother is out of service.
Thank you for waiting, that father you have
    reached is a temporary disconnect.

I'm sorry that landlord is not in working order.
Please verify your neighborhood and try it
    again.
I'm sorry those repairs are out of service.
Thank you for waiting, that official you have
    reached is not reachable at this time.

I'm sorry that water is not in drinking order.
Please verify that sunlight and try it later.
I'm sorry that blue sky is out of service.
Thank you for waiting, those flowers and trees
    are permanently disconnected.

I'm sorry that country is not in working order.
I'm sorry that planet is out of service.
Please verify that godhead and try much later.
Thank you for waiting, that universe has been
    dis——

                    —Eve Merriam

    The child who has been one of six little mice sitting down
to spin or the ghost who "screams like a storm at sea" is
learning to know the great expanse of the world of poetry.

And when middle graders provide voices for the world network of machines, they learn that poems can make a sharp commentary about our communications network and reach into every aspect of our lives.

5 Bringing It All Together

FOR EVERY poem suggested in this book, there are hundreds—even thousands—more that appeal to young readers and listeners and may draw them into active involvement. Finding such poems can become a sort of treasure hunt for older children and teenagers. Once they have had experience with poetry—hearing it and "doing it"—they are eager to find new treasure.

What they come up with may be as simple as the old folk song "Poor Old Lady, She Swallowed a Fly."

Or it may have the dramatic swing of "The Highwayman" by Alfred Noyes or "Sea Fever" by John Masefield.

Or it may have the grim heroics of "Casablanca" by Felicia Hemans, which begins:

> The boy stood on the burning deck
>> Whence all but he had fled;
> The flame that lit the battle's wreck
>> Shone round him o'er the dead.

Experienced poetry readers frequently enjoy "doing" a poem individually—that is, reading the poem aloud to others without music, movement, or dramatics. This takes a bit of practice, but readers and listeners enjoy the search for the right poem and then bringing it to others.

I once heard a thirteen-year-old dog lover ask to read his favorite poem—one he had been practicing with a tape recorder for several days. It was "Lone Dog" by Irene Rutherford McLeod, which begins:

> I'm a lean dog, a keen dog, a wild dog, and
>   lone;
> I'm a rough dog, a tough dog, hunting on my
>   own;
> I'm a bad dog, a mad dog, teasing silly
>   sheep . . .

His listeners were spellbound. In a few days, another student asked to read "my favorite poem." This time it was a cat poem, "The Rum Tum Tugger," from *Old Possum's Book of Practical Cats* by T. S. Eliot. Several in the group had seen the musical based on these poems and the following day brought in a tape of the show. For the next week T. S. Eliot and his cats took over.

As children meet different poems and experiment with ways of presenting them to their friends, new ideas and new techniques emerge: chanting a poem while background music is being played perhaps, using a tape recorder to provide appropriate sound effects, showing slides to establish the setting, creating a puppet show to dramatize a poem, making a video of the performance, or any combination of these.

Frequently, background music adds to the poem's appeal. It may be a song that one group can hum while another reads the lines of the poem. But it has to be the right song, and children become expert in making a choice.

101

The old spiritual "One Wide River" seems the perfect accompaniment for *Prayers from the Ark*. "Kum ba ya" makes a lovely background for the reading of several poems by Langston Hughes, such as "The Dream Keeper" and "April Rain Song." "Take Me Out to the Ball Game" fits the narrative poem "Casey at the Bat" and other baseball poems.

As a poem is read, children hum the melody softly. As the reading ends, the humming chorus can break into the words of the song for an effective finale.

One of the most stirring segments of a poetry hour in which I have taken part was the time a New York City teacher taught a group of us to sing the "Fivefold Amen." "Pronounce it *AY-min*!" she said. So we sang: "AY-min! AY-min! AY-min! AY-min! AY-min!" Then she suggested we hum it while she read "Mother to Son" by Langston Hughes.

"And at the end," she said, "sing out the words of the Fivefold AY-min!" Without further rehearsal, we were swept into the emotional impact of poem and music.

Recordings can be used for a musical background, too, and here there are many possibilities: recordings of songs and dances of American Indians to use with their poems; music from Africa and Latin America. Fourth and fifth graders will listen to one recording after another in their search for the right one to use with a favorite poem.

Playing a record, humming, singing, chanting, body movement, and drama may sometimes be combined to accompany the reading of a poem or a group of poems.

One sixth-grade teacher tells of playing a part of Dvorak's "New World" Symphony as she read Aileen Fisher's long poem *In the Middle of the Night*. Then she asked students to pretend they were taking a walk in the middle of the night as she read the poem with the musical background. When someone suggested it would be better if the room were darkened, blinds were drawn and lights turned off, so that music and words could cast their spell.

With a little encouragement, children begin to search out poems on the same theme and weave them into a sequence to present at the next story hour. It may be a combination of poems by one writer—Eve Merriam and Shel Silverstein are always favorites in something of this sort—or perhaps a group of scary poems or funny poems.

One group of fourth graders planned a poetry hour about the theme "Who Am I?" using Felice Holman's poem of that title* as a starter. They went on to include David McCord's "This Is My Rock"** and Emily Dickinson's "I'm nobody. Who are you?"*** They used background music and some chanting of lines and repeated phrases.

It was a very stirring little poetry series—perhaps more serious than most adults would have considered for this age level, but it was the children's own and deeply moving to them.

Folk tales, poems, and music from Africa can be woven into a beautiful production, perhaps with a recording of African drums in the background. A Christmas program might include several of Eleanor Farjeon's Christmas poems read over the humming of traditional carols, the Russian folk tale of Babushka, and then "The Twelve Days of Christmas" with everyone chiming in.

Often such a mini-program grows into a multimedia production including pantomime and dance with music and colored slides. Poems written by students can be read along with those of published poets. Slides of the children's paintings may become the perfect visual setting.

There is no limit to the imaginative use of poetry with

* From Felice Holman, *At the Top of My Voice and Other Poems* (Scribner, 1970).

** From David McCord, *Far and Few: Rhymes of the Never Was and Always Is* (Little, Brown, 1953).

*** From *Poems of Emily Dickinson*, selected by Helen Plotz (Crowell, 1964).

children. As they listen and chime in, invent movements and characters, and use song and dance to respond to the words, they expand the writer's original vision and create their own new worlds, truly growing up with poetry.

Directory of Collections by Individual Poets

Poetry Collections by Those Whose Work Is Included in This Book

Bodecker, N. M.
Carrot Holes and Frisbee Trees. 48 pp. Macmillan, 1983.
It's Raining Said John Twaining. Unpaged. Macmillan, 1977.
Snowman Sniffles and Other Verse. 80 pp. Macmillan, 1981.

Brooks, Gwendolyn
Bronzeville Boys and Girls. 48 pp. Harper, 1956.

Brown, Margaret Wise
Nibble, Nibble. Unpaged. Harper, 1959.
Where Have You Been? 32 pp. Hastings, 1952.

Carroll, Lewis
Humorous Verse of Lewis Carroll. 446 pp. Dover, 1933.
Jabberwocky. 32 pp. A. Whitman, 1985.

Ciardi, John
Doodle Soup. 64 pp. Houghton, 1985.
I Met a Man. Houghton, 1973.
The Reason for the Pelican. 63 pp. Contemporary Books, 1989.
You Read to Me, I'll Read to You. 64 pp. Harper, 1961.

de Gasztold, Carmen Bernos
Prayers from the Ark and The Creatures Choir. 128 pp. Penguin, 1976.

de la Mare, Walter
Peacock Pie: A Book of Rhymes. 107 pp. Faber, 1988.
Rhymes and Verses: Collected Poems for Young People. 368 pp. Holt, 1988.
Songs of Childhood. 106 pp. Dover, 1968.

de Regniers, Beatrice Schenk
May I Bring a Friend? Macmillan, 1964.
A Week in the Life of Best Friends and Other Poems of Friendship. 48 pp. Macmillan, 1986.

Eastwick, Ivy O.
In and Out the Windows: Happy Poems for Childhood. Plough, 1969.

Eliot, T. S.
Old Possum's Book of Practical Cats. 56 pp. Harcourt, 1968.

Farjeon, Eleanor
Eleanor Farjeon's Poems for Children. 256 pp. Harper, 1984.

Fisher, Aileen
The House of a Mouse. 32 pp. Harper, 1988.
Listen, Rabbit. Unpaged. Harper, 1964.
Rabbits, Rabbits. 32 pp. Harper, 1983.
When It Comes to Bugs. 32 pp. Harper, 1986.

Fleischman, Paul
I Am Phoenix: Poems for Two Voices. 51 pp. Harper, 1985.

Joyful Noise: Poems for Two Voices. 44 pp. Harper, 1988.

Fyleman, Rose
Fairy Went A-Marketing. 24 pp. Dutton, 1986.

Hoberman, Mary Ann
The Cozy Book. 48 pp. Penguin, 1982.
A House Is a House for Me. 48 pp. Penguin, 1978.

Holman, Felice
The Song in My Head and Other Poems. 64 pp. Macmillan, 1985.

Hubbell, Patricia
The Tiger Brought Pink Lemonade. 32 pp. Macmillan, 1988.

Hughes, Langston
The Dream Keeper. (Grades 7–11.) 77 pp. Knopf, 1962.

Knight, Joan
Tickle-Toe Rhymes. 32 pp. Orchard Books, 1989.

Kuskin, Karla
Dogs and Dragons, Trees and Dreams. 96 pp. Harper, 1980.
Near the Window Tree: Poems and Notes. 64 pp. Harper, 1975.
Something Sleeping in the Hall. 64 pp. Harper, 1985.

Lindsay, Vachel
Johnny Appleseed and Other Poems. 138 pp. Harmony Raine, 1981.

Livingston, Myra Cohn
Birthday Poems. 32 pp. Holiday, 1989.
Higgledy-Piggledy: Verses and Pictures. 32 pp. Macmillan, 1986.
Monkey Puzzle and Other Poems. 64 pp. Macmillan, 1984.
Worlds I Know and Other Poems. 32 pp. Macmillan, 1987.

Martin, Bill Jr. and John Archambault
Barn Dance. Unpaged. Holt, 1986.

McCord, David

Every Time I Climb a Tree. (K–3.) 48 pp. Little, Brown, 1967.

One at a Time: Collected Poems for the Young. 494 pp. Little, Brown, 1978.

Speak Up: More Rhymes of the Never Was and Always Is. 80 pp. Little, Brown, 1980.

Merriam, Eve

Blackberry Ink. 40 pp. Morrow, 1985.

Chortles. 60 pp. Morrow, 1989.

Fresh Paint: New Poems. 48 pp. Macmillan, 1986.

Halloween ABC. 32 pp. Macmillan, 1987.

Jamboree. 96 pp. Dell, 1984.

A Poem for a Pickle. 40 pp. Morrow, 1989.

A Sky Full of Poems. 101 pp. Dell, 1986.

You Be Good and I'll Be Night: Jump-on-the-Bed Poems. 40 pp. Morrow, 1988.

Nichol, bp

Once: A Lullaby. 24 pp. Greenwillow, 1986.

Rossetti, Christina

Goblin Market. 48 pp. Godine, 1984.

Sing Song: A Nursery Rhyme Book. 130 pp. Dover, 1969.

Silverstein, Shel

A Light in the Attic. 176 pp. Harper, 1981.

Where the Sidewalk Ends. 166 pp. Harper, 1974.

Watson, Clyde

Catch Me & Kiss Me & Say It Again. 64 pp. Putnam, 1983.

Father Fox's Penny Rhymes. 64 pp. Harper, 1987.

Directory of Anthologies of Poetry for Children

Each contains the work of many poets

Favorite Poems Old and New, selected by Helen Ferris. An all-inclusive collection for all ages from all periods. 595 pp. Doubleday, 1957.

I Am the Darker Brother: An Anthology of Modern Poems by Negro Americans, edited by Arnold Adoff. 139 pp. Macmillan, 1968.

I Like You, If You Like Me: Poems of Friendship, selected by Myra Cohn Livingston. 143 pp. Ninety poems from many periods and many cultures tell of the joys, pitfalls, and importance of friendship. Macmillan, 1987.

. . . I never saw another butterfly . . . Children's Drawings and Poems from Theresienstadt Concentration Camp 1942–1944, edited by Hans Volavkova. 80 pp. Schocken, n.d.

In a Spring Garden, selected by Richard Lewis. Twenty-three haiku dramatically illustrated by Ezra Jack Keats. 32 pp. Dial, 1965.

Knock at a Star: A Child's Introduction to Poetry by X. J. Kennedy and Dorothy M. Kennedy. Over 150 poems—lively, interesting, funny—are woven into an explanation of the how and what of poetry. 148 pp. Little, Brown, 1982.

The Music of What Happens: Poems That Tell Stories, selected by Paul Janeczko. Grade 8 up. 208 pp. Orchard Books, 1988.

My Black Me: A Beginning Book of Black Poetry, edited by Arnold Adoff. Fifty poems by twenty-five black poets. 83 pp. Dutton, 1974.

A New Treasury of Children's Poetry, selected and introduced by Joanna Cole. Over 200 traditional and modern poems, nonsense rhymes, and limericks. 224 pp. Doubleday, 1984.

Piping Down the Valleys Wild, compiled by Nancy Larrick. 250 choice poems for family reading. 271 pp. Delacorte, 1968. Dell paperback, 1985.

Poems to Read to the Very Young, selected by Josette Frank. Forty little poems with charming illustrations by Dagmar Wilson. Unpaged. Random House, 1961. Paperback.

The Poetry Troupe: Poems to Read Aloud, compiled by Isabel Wilner. Wonderful material for group reading and chanting. 223 pp. Macmillan, 1977.

The Random House Book of Poetry for Children: A Treasury of 572 Poems for Today's Child, compiled by Jack Prelutsky. Illustrated by Arnold Lobel. A sumptuous collection. 248 pp. Random House, 1983.

Read-Aloud Rhymes for the Very Young, selected by Jack Prelutsky. More than 200 sparkling verses for every occasion. 98 pp. Alfred A. Knopf, 1986.

Sing a Song of Popcorn, selected by Beatrice Schenk de-Regniers et al.; illustrated by nine Caldecott Medal artists. 129 favorite poems—funny, touching, spine-tingling, with magnificent full-color illustrations. First published in 1969 under the title *Poems Children Will Sit Still For.* The new edition, *Sing a Song of Popcorn,* was published by Scholastic, 1988. 160 pp.

Surprises, easy-to-read poems selected by Lee Bennett Hopkins. A delightful collection for beginning readers. 64 pp. Harper, 1984.

Talking to the Sun: An Illustrated Anthology of Poems for Young People, selected and introduced by Kenneth Koch and Kate Farrell. 180 poems, verses, chants of many nations, many cultures; illustrated with treasures from the Metropolitan Museum of Art. 112 pp. The Metropolitan Museum of Art and Holt, Rinehart and Winston, 1985.

This Delicious Day: Sixty-Five Poems, compiled by Paul Janeczko. (Grades 4–6.) 96 pp. Orchard Books, 1987.

When the Dark Comes Dancing: The Bedtime Poetry Book, compiled by Nancy Larrick. Poems and lullabies with notes for parents. 79 pp. Philomel, 1983.

Author and
Title Index

First Line Index

Subject Index

About the Author

NANCY LARRICK—teacher, writer, lecturer, and editor—has become a driving force in converting today's children into poetry buffs. She has compiled twenty anthologies of poetry for young people, all with the help of the children themselves. Seven of her anthologies have become mass market paperbacks, and many have been listed as ALA Notable Books.

For a number of years she directed the Poetry Workshop at Lehigh University, where parents and teachers experimented with ways of introducing children and poetry happily. *Let's Do a Poem!* is a direct outgrowth of the workshop.

Today millions of parents know Nancy Larrick as the author of *A Parent's Guide to Children's Reading,* first published in 1958. By this time the book is in its fifth completely revised edition and has sold over a million and a quarter copies.

Nancy Larrick grew up in Winchester, Virginia, graduated from Goucher College, received her master's degree from Columbia University and her doctorate from New York University. She was one of the founders of the International Reading Association and its second president.